Dear Model Cir Lan,

Jillian to the Rescue

Thanks for all you do for me and Ted.
Love you kid !

Jillian to the Rescue!

Book One: Lost and Found

By Wendy Tinker

Cover Illustration by Marian Duncan

Published by Bargello Books
PO Box 1287, McKenna Washington 98558

First Edition February 2019

ISBN: 978-1-7336-5651-1

Disclaimer: While some characters and locations in this
novel are based on real people and places, none of the
events in this book actually took place.

DEDICATION

This book is dedicated to all the people who work tirelessly to rehome and rescue horses every day in the United States and around the world, and to the horses and donkeys that still manage to show unconditional love even after years of mistreatment.

If only one life is saved by someone who reads this book then my purpose is fulfilled.

Author's Note: I am pleased to donate 10% of my gross proceeds to registered non-profit horse rescues across the United States. So, thank you. You have just helped to save a horse through the purchase of this book! Visit www.bargellobooks.com to learn more.

TABLE OF CONTENTS

PROLOGUE   1
CHAPTER 1 - Nothing is the Same   3
CHAPTER 2 - Chaos and Confusion   10
CHAPTER 3 - Decisions, Decisions   21
CHAPTER 4 - A New Day   32
CHAPTER 5 - Jealousy   43
CHAPTER 6 - What's A Jibbah?   50
CHAPTER 7 - Rescue 101   60
CHAPTER 8 - Mean Girls, Nice Boys   65
CHAPTER 9 - Heartstrings   73
CHAPTER 10 - A Poopy Tale   84
CHAPTER 11 - Hoof Picks, Horns & Horses   90
CHAPTER 12 - A Wild Ride   98
CHAPTER 13 - Freedom at Last!   107
CHAPTER 14 - Unhappy Trails   113
CHAPTER 15 - A Sticky Situation   122
CHAPTER 16 - Truth Be Told   128
CHAPTER 17 - Introductions   135
CHAPTER 18 - Ride 'em Cowboy!   140
CHAPTER 19 - Eight Seconds   148
CHAPTER 20 - Friends, Food & Mystery   154
CHAPTER 21 - Investigations   162
CHAPTER 22 - Questions Answered   171
CHAPTER 23 - The Good, The Bad & The Ugly   181
CHAPTER 24 - Touch and Go   189
CHAPTER 25 - Waiting Game   198
CHAPTER 26 - The Gifts of Giving   207

ACKNOWLEDGEMENTS

I cannot thank the following people enough for their love and support as I researched and wrote this book. First and foremost my sister, Gena Sansone, without whose inspiration and encouragement I wouldn't have even started. To Vicki Hughes, my friend since childhood, I can't express my complete gratitude for the hours you spent editing proof after proof and offering invaluable advice. Thanks so much to Candice Cassidy who performed the final edit on my story is such a way that my style stayed true and my many exclamation points removed. To my beta readers for their input and enthusiasm, thank you.

I'd also like to thank the horses that have touched my life since childhood and shown me their unconditional love: My Fair Lady, the part-Arabian mare that sparked my love of Arabian horses, Cherokey's Leah, Dana Diego, Drama Dot Com LRA, Sultan's Great Endying, Bargello's Razoul, Chianti LRA, Bargello's Illuminati, WH Sassheikhin, Bargello's Pele, Bargello's Poseiidon, ForeReal, Fire and Lace CAHR, Demaraz Classic, Urban Legend ST, Tiffany Grace, Urban Myth, Legendary ST. And rescue horses: Bargello's Bolt A Fire, Bargello's Amazing Grace, A Lil Bueno Honey, Tessa and Donny, Sassy, Araabella, PA Heiress. You have all enriched my life in such a way that words cannot express. I love you all.

PROLOGUE

The horses stood in the mid-day heat heads hanging, eyes dull. The tattered remains of their shade cover did nothing to shield them from the blistering rays of the Arizona sun. It had been days since they'd been fed or watered. Bones showed through rough hides, stretched thin and dry. Several of the herd were already dead. The harsh desert had taken its toll.

The grey mare raised her head nostril flared, scenting change. The abandoned mobile home squatted helplessly nearby, its crippled door squeaking with each gust of the rising wind. Something moved in the grass: a snake, or a rabbit. She pricked her ears toward the movement, listening carefully, but heard just the sound of the wind gathering strength and speed.

She turned her attention to her grown daughter who lay exhausted and emaciated at her feet. The chestnut filly made no attempt to rise. She lay eyes closed, knees tucked under her chest, chin to the ground. Resignation showed in every movement. The young mare sighed. Her dam nuzzled her with encouragement, but hope had faded.

The rising wind that swept down the mountain slope buffeted the tattered cover and the rusted slabs of corrugated roofing that hung precariously above the pen. The grey mare turned her back to the gusts as they gathered strength, trying to shield her prostrate offspring.

The door banged on the mobile home. Sand swirled. The impulsive wind swooped under the flimsy shelter, knocking it sideways and sending the corrugated roof onto the horses below.

The grey mare screamed and bolted. Her daughter, unable to flee, lay captive. Her struggles futile. Her fate sealed.

CHAPTER 1 - Nothing is the Same

Jillian's eyes flew open. Her heart pounding. The unfamiliar feel of the room, the hum of air conditioning left her gulping for breath until her mind caught up with her body and she remembered where she was. Her head, half lifted off the pillow, fell back, and she rolled on her side in a fetal position where she wanted to stay forever.

She wasn't home. She was in Arizona at Grandma Allison's. Memories flowed unbidden and she couldn't stop the tears. Her parents. The car crash. Her life had ended when theirs did. Everything she knew and loved was gone, and in this broiling hot town outside of Phoenix, she was supposed to go on living. Jillian flopped to her other side to face the wall, legs tangled in the cotton sheets. She hated it here.

Three weeks ago Jillian had arrived in New River, Arizona. It was a nasty, unforgiving, and unfriendly place. Everything was sharp and vicious and either bit or poked you. It was so different from home. She ached for her shady, cool backyard in Woodinville, Washington, with its lush, green lawns where the tall pine trees helped her play hide-and-seek with her friends. She could walk through the forest in a downpour and barely get wet. Jillian loved the piney smell of the soft forest floor. She wanted to lie in her favorite spot in the woods and look up at patches of deep blue sky through the tall trees and feel protected again. She wanted to play with her neighbors, Janet and Andy, in the fort her dad had built.

Her dad... The thought of him brought more tears. How could she keep living like everything was going to be okay? Who would tuck her in and call her "Jilly Bean" and "Tresses?" Who would help her with her math homework now that Mom was gone? No one. No one at all. It certainly wouldn't be Grandma Allison. She had tried to be accommodating with Jillian, but Grandma spent several days a week volunteering at the food bank, and she had her routine. Jillian didn't feel like she fit into it. Not at all. And Uncle Aaron wasn't going to help her. He thought she was a burden they didn't need; he'd made that clear on the first day of her arrival.

That day was a blur, landing at the airport in Phoenix with only her two suitcases and backpack. It hadn't been her first flight, but it was the only time in her twelve years she had ever flown alone. She felt scared and insecure when the flight attendant accompanied her off the plane down to baggage claim where Grandma Allison and Uncle Aaron were waiting. She didn't recognize anyone at first, and for a fleeting moment, she had a paralyzing fear that instantly turned to hope. Maybe they had changed their minds and she could turn around and get on the plane and fly back to Seattle? Maybe they didn't want her and she could live with Janet and Andy? She brightened for a moment. But before long, a slender, grey-haired woman smiled at her and reached out her arms to attempt a hug.

She had only met her grandmother once before at Christmas when she was eight. She remembered her gentle smile and the soft peppermint candies she kept in her pocket in a little ziplock baggie. Her grandma would sneak them to Jillian when she thought her parents weren't looking. She appeared much older now and far shorter than Jillian remembered, but she still had that gentle look. Jillian held back at first, but those kind powdery-blue eyes, brimming with tears, compelled Jillian to accept her embrace. The attendant looked away, blinking at the raw emotion between the two, a grey-haired, deeply tanned woman and a thin young girl with a mop of red curls and a swath of freckles across her white face.

Jillian had never met Uncle Aaron, but she saw a bit of her mother in his chocolate-colored eyes and dark brown hair. But his sullen, disinterested look wasn't like her mom at all. He was busy studying the carpet and watching passengers and the baggage carousel, keeping his eyes averted trying to ignore the two of them. He started to edge away but Grandma Allison called him to meet his niece, and he turned and appraised Jillian.

"I'm Aaron, your uncle. Sorry about… you know," he trailed awkwardly. "Your mom was a lot older than me and, uh, I didn't know her that well." Again he paused and looked down. "So, which bags are yours?" he asked, turning to the carousel and ending the one-sided conversation.

When Jillian stepped out of the terminal, she was met with a blast of heat that almost stopped her. It felt like it did when she stood too close to the flames in front of their big fireplace in the living room in Washington. The skin on her face tightened and she stopped short, earning a curious stare from Uncle Aaron.

"What's wrong? Never felt our 'dry heat' before?" he chuckled, shaking his head. Grandma Allison frowned at him and took her hand.

"You'll get used to it, honey, I promise," she said to Jillian, who was positive she would never get used to the awful heat—ever.

The hour-long drive in traffic up Highway 17 took them north from the city of Phoenix to a little blip off the freeway. Sitting in the desert, New River, Arizona, was a cactus-filled landscape, peppered with single-story houses and rutted dirt roads. There was a town called Anthem not far away, and she was going to be enrolled in school there. It was hard enough moving to a strange place without also having to deal with attending classes that were almost over and meeting new kids in a school she didn't know anything about.

Her grandma's house turned out to be a single level, southwestern style building that was almost a mile up a dirt road in the middle of nowhere. The nearest neighbor was over a little hill, and if she stood on the front porch, she could see miles and miles of empty desert that looked as dry and desolate as she felt inside. The contrast to her suburban home in Washington was so stark, it was as if she were living on a different planet. Green versus brown, rain versus sun, cool versus hot, friendly versus lonely; it could not be a single bit more different from her family's home in the Pacific Northwest.

When they'd arrived, Jillian was shown to her bedroom. It had blank, white walls and a tan tiled floor. Her uncle brought in her suitcases and set them in the middle of her room.

"You're lucky we have room. If ole Johnny hadn't gotten hurt and moved to a nursing home, this room woulda' still been rented. Costing us too," he muttered under his breath at the end.

The room was small with a scuffed wood dresser in the corner and a twin bed with no headboard and new sheets. They obviously knew nothing about her, or they would never have put pink sheets on her bed. She hated pink.

Jillian flipped back over to face her room, frowning. She could hear Uncle Aaron in the kitchen complaining to Grandma Allison. He seemed to complain a lot. She wasn't sure what he did for work, but he often slept in late, left the house around midday, and came home at dinner time. He rarely talked to her, and she had an unexplainable sense he resented her. For what reason, she had no clue.

Groaning, Jillian sat up on her bed, pulling up her knees and hugging them. It was Sunday on the last weekend before she had to go to school. They'd taken her shopping at the outlet mall in Anthem yesterday for school clothes and supplies. She'd learned that Grandma Allison didn't drive and any time they needed to go shopping or do anything, they had to rely on Uncle Aaron to take them. It was an unpleasant arrangement since Aaron always griped about how much time it was going to take, even before they got started.

Aaron had dropped them off and left to sulk somewhere while she and Grandma bought some clothes. It took a couple of hours and was weird having her grandma inspect her choices and shake her head at price tags. Jillian felt like nothing but a giant burden. She watched wistfully as girls and their mom's tried on clothes and giggled at inside jokes while they browsed the aisles together. It was depressing.

Leaving her bed, Jillian took a deep breath, letting it out with a sigh. On her last day of freedom before school, she was going to do a little exploring before getting her clothes and supplies ready for tomorrow. Jillian heard her grandma call her from the kitchen, "Come on out, honey, breakfast is ready." She dressed and headed out to eat.

"Don't you look nice in those shorts, Jillian," Grandma Allison exclaimed over her new purchase. "What do you want to do today?" she asked, raising her thin eyebrows and looking at the girl. "Aaron will be taking me to the food bank for a few hours, but I should be back by lunch. If you want to go outside, it's best to do it soon before it gets hot."

That last comment almost made Jillian snort out the orange juice she was drinking. "You mean before you can cook an egg on the sidewalk, right?" replied Jillian, her first attempt at humor since her arrival.

Grandma looked at her with a quick smile. "I suppose you're right, it must seem that way to you, but I swear you'll get used to it. It just takes a while.

And when the winter comes, you'll be in heaven," she added, rolling her eyes in a blissful expression. Jillian giggled a little and was rewarded with another grin.

Uncle Aaron barged through the back door into the kitchen. "There's a bunch a people over at Ole Hank's place, Ma. Do you reckon they're finally taking away them horses they got up there?" he asked. "Since he passed, that kid of his hardly feeds 'em, and they stink up the place. I hope they're getting rid of all of 'em."

Jillian asked, "What horses are they, Uncle Aaron? I didn't know the neighbor had horses."

"Nah," said Aaron, "you're thinking of Bill's place over the hill next door. No, Hank lived up the road, around the corner. You musta' not been up there yet," he explained. "He used to breed fancy horses for years, but the last five years he couldn't do the work and, well, you can't hardly find anyone that helps very good anymore. Then he died and his kid is supposed to be taking care of 'em," he added with a sneer. "Hope they kill all them stinky things. Get 'em outta here."

Curiosity piqued, and feeling a shot of empathy for the horses who, like her, were in their circumstances because of death, she asked, "Grandma, can I go and look? I won't get in the way."

Her grandmother searched her face, seeing a spark of light that hadn't been there before and replied, "Of course, honey. Just be careful and stay out of the way. Horses can be dangerous. And if Hank's family hasn't been taking such good care of them, it might not be what you really want to see."

Jillian jumped up from the table before her grandmother changed her mind. She cleared her empty cereal bowl and left the house, heading down the driveway to see what was going on up the road.

"Watch for snakes!" her grandma called as she left.

CHAPTER 2 - Chaos and Confusion

The dirt road wound up past the driveway and between two hills. As Jillian trudged along, already feeling the heat, she looked with some interest at the desert that surrounded her. She saw the desolate terrain through her only reference, that of her childhood home, where tall pines and lush greens had given her comfort and safety. This tainted view exposed only the dry and dangerous parts of the desert.

Snakes. Great. Another nasty thing that bites and hurts you. She kept her eyes on the dirt in front of her. "Jumping" cholla cactus lined the road threatening to attack with their two-inch, barbed needles that could sense the heat of a potential target. Her uncle said the cactus would actually let their needles loose and could "jump" several inches to embed themselves in an unsuspecting victim. Jillian didn't believe him, but she had no desire to test how far a cholla could jump if they could actually "jump" at all; she gave them a wide berth.

The saguaro cactus, spreading their huge limbs at crazy angles, dwarfed the chollas. If Jillian had to like one type of cactus in Arizona, she supposed it was the saguaro. Each one was different: some had loads of branches that looked like arms reaching up to the unending sun. Others had branches that curved, and some even pointed to the ground. At the end of their driveway stood two saguaro's that had grown together so that one looked like it was cradling the other in its arms. But they too had long spikes and she kept her distance, appreciating them from as far away as possible.

Dozens of varieties of scrubby plants and cacti filled the desert with their spines and spikes and needles and pokey parts. The short walk up the hill cemented her belief that

Arizona was the driest, meanest, most dusty, painful place in the world.

Rounding the bend, Jillian stopped short as she reached the driveway. She understood what her uncle was saying about a crowd. There were three trucks and trailers as well as a beat-up sedan and a bunch of people milling about near a round pen. The property was a mess, with garbage piled in heaps and paddocks made of rusted three-rail panels tied together with baling string. A lopsided, single-wide mobile home sat off to the side, and the run-down property was surrounded with an assortment of metal posts and wooden stakes holding up a bent wire fence on the verge of collapse.

They caught her eye immediately—eight or nine skinny horses pacing in the dilapidated corral. Nearby, a pretty woman with shoulder-length dark blonde hair was talking to a skinny young man in a grease-covered baseball cap. She looked like the person in charge. Jillian couldn't hear them, but the man kept shaking his head in answer to her questions. Two other women and two men were standing around the corral watching the horses and waiting for the go-ahead to get them loaded in the horse trailers.

Not knowing whether or not she should announce her arrival, Jillian stepped off the driveway and found a boulder where she could sit and watch the scene unfold. She guessed that Old Hank's relative was the guy with the white tank and greasy cap that the woman was talking to. He kept rubbing his arms, shaking his head, and looking at the ground as she asked him questions. Jillian could see the woman tense, her lips forming a hard line after every shake of his baseball cap.

The property looked abandoned. The door to the mobile home was hanging on its hinges and seemed like it hadn't been opened in a while. The smell of horse manure was overpowering. Usually, Jillian kind of liked the smell of horses, but this was different. There was something else. A darker, rancid scent. It didn't smell healthy.

Just beyond the corral was a faded cover made out of tent-type material ripped and shredded by the wind and sun. It attempted to cover a pen, which was knee-deep in horse manure, whose former shelter was now just a careless pile of corrugated roofing that had fallen in a heap. The fencing around the pen ran in a crazy crooked line. It didn't look at all safe for horses.

Turning her attention to the horses in the round corral, Jillian felt an ache. She could see every rib. The helpers had filled the water trough in the corral, and all the animals were pushing their way to the fresh water. Their listless eyes had brightened at the sight. Their heads seemed too big for their necks and they had a kind of scoop to their faces. It made their eyes seem huge. All but one grey mare was greedily drinking from the trough. Instead, she stood staring at her old enclosure.

All of a sudden, everybody started moving. Jillian missed something. The backs of the trailers were opened and the two men entered the paddock. The skinny guy reseated his grimy hat and shoved a signed paper into the woman's hands, then beat a hasty retreat to his dented sedan. Gravel flew as he sped out, as if trying to leave his guilty conscience behind with the horses.

Despite the sudden noise, the horses stayed docile, and it didn't take the handlers long to get halters on all of them before putting them in the trailers. It all was going smoothly, except for the grey mare who kept refusing to load. It took the two men and a pair of ropes across the horse's butt to get her on the last trailer. She clattered on in a rush, screaming her indignity and rolling her eyes in fear and frustration.

Jillian felt a connection to the poor horse that just wanted to stay where she was and didn't want to get on the trailer. Why would she want to leave everything that she knew, even if what she knew wasn't great? Change was scary.

As the trucks and trailers left in a swirl of dust and exhaust, no one seemed to notice her sitting on the boulder. Feeling insignificant, she watched them go. The ripping pain of her parents' death returned as she remembered how the police had arrived while she was making beaded bracelets on the floor at Janet's house just a month and a half ago.

Mrs. Jenkins had found the girls in Janet's room, and she asked Janet to wait for a minute and brought Jillian into the living room. Jillian thought it was odd because Mrs. Jenkins had never separated them before. She wondered for a second if they'd done something wrong.

When she entered the living room she saw two police officers standing next to the fireplace. *What were they doing there, and what did it have to do with me?* Mrs. Jenkins sat her on the couch and sunk down next to her wrapping her arm around Jillian's shoulder. Then, the bigger of the two cops knelt in front of her and took off his hat. He said his name was Officer McCall. She noticed his eyebrows were reddish and bushy but that he was bald underneath his hat. He looked into her eyes and she could see his eyes were shiny. Then he started talking.

He told her that her parents had been in an accident on the commute home from their jobs. He explained they had been blindsided by a vehicle that had swerved into their lane as they exited the freeway. They were killed instantly. There would be an investigation and the insurance company had been called. Everyone was very, very sorry. The officer told her a social worker was on the way and she would explain more about what was going to happen next.

Jillian could see that the officer was talking, his lips were moving and he was looking her in the face, but she couldn't hear him clearly. It was totally bizarre. She felt like she wasn't in her body, and that even though Officer McCall was speaking directly to her, it wasn't really her, but just some unfortunate girl she didn't know. Jillian was floating near the ceiling looking down at the bouncy red curls that topped the thin shoulders of that poor girl, feeling sorry for her. Then in a whoosh, she was back in her body and she could see the officer's bushy eyebrows over his hazel eyes, but this time they were knitted together in concern.

"Are you okay? Just breathe. Can you do that for me? Take a deep breath," he inhaled in example.

The reality of what the officer had said struck her like a blow. Her parents were dead. Hers, not some poor girl. Mrs. Jenkins reached out and gathered her up and Jillian cried and cried. The worst thing in the world had happened.

The woman from social services arrived half an hour later. By then, Janet and Andy had heard the news, and Mr. Jenkins was on his way home from work. The state worker introduced herself as Ms. Thomas. *She has the prettiest skin*, Jillian couldn't help but admiring. It was so smooth, and a light brown—or more like the creamy color of her mother's morning coffee. The woman's hair was tied back, her brown eyes intelligent and compassionate. Ms. Thomas explained that the police had contacted her parent's work and gotten in touch with her next of kin, which was her grandmother. The social worker asked if her Grandma Allison and Uncle Aaron were her only blood relatives. Jillian didn't know, but she hadn't ever heard of any other cousins or family. Her dad had been an only child like she was. Ms. Thomas said she would take care of everything, and then she and the Jenkins's went into the kitchen to finish the conversation.

Jillian was able to stay with the Jenkins family for the three weeks that it took to arrange the funeral. In retrospect, it seemed like she'd spent a lot of that time floating out of her body, seeing herself grieve and cry, watching herself show the police where her parents kept their important papers, and answering questions from her parents' lawyer and friend, Mr. Steiner. Not much of what anyone said stuck with her. Jillian found in the beginning, when she felt overwhelmed, she could retreat to the ceiling and she wouldn't feel things so deeply. It was as if she was only skimming through the surface of her life. Unfortunately, that odd ability faded after a couple weeks. She tried to tune out her feelings but it got harder as they days passed.

Several times during those first weeks she had strong, clear feelings that it was all a huge mistake. There was nothing wrong, her parents were fine, and she was having a horrible dream. She would wake up and everything would be back to normal: her mom would make her yogurt with strawberries and granola, and her parents would joke about their "Date-ly Commute," laughing about how lucky they were to go on two dates a day, five days a week as they drove back and forth to work together.

But the awful dream kept going on, and then there was the funeral with hundreds of people, most of whom she didn't know. Grandma Allison had the flu and she and Uncle Aaron couldn't attend, so on that Saturday in early March—in the big Protestant church where her mom sometimes went—Jillian discovered the truth of her situation.

The truth was that she was alone. The Jenkins's had been great to her. Mrs. Jenkins tried not to cry when she tucked the girls in every night, and Mr. Jenkins was solemn but kind. Janet and Andy did their best to distract and keep her busy, but they could never understand what being alone really was because they had each other. That feeling of loneliness enveloped her again as she sat on the boulder in the Arizona morning sun.

She sagged on her perch, tears coursing tracks down her dusty cheeks. She was wondering why she was chosen to be a kid who lost her parents and have her heart torn from her chest. Jillian sat staring out at the desert wondering if she would ever feel like she was a part of anything ever again and wishing she could float outside herself as she had been able to when she first lost them.

A sudden noise stirred her from her reverie. She lifted her head, tilting it toward the corral. There it was again: something like a snuffle. Wondering if she was imagining things, Jillian walked up the drive and looked into the corral. It was empty of all but trash and sand. The ragged cover flapped in the breeze over the fenced area, and as she paused, she heard it again: a sound like a ragged breath or a sob. Jillian turned toward the noise and walked on.

She stopped a few yards later wondering if she was imagining things after all and thinking that it might be against the law to be on the property. She was about to turn and leave when she heard it one more time. The sound was coming from the hillside in the pen with the flapping cover. She picked her way through the rubbish and opened the rickety metal gate. The noise came from under the heap of corrugated roofing panels.

Jillian paused again, this time feeling a spark of fear. She wondered what lived in the desert that would make a noise like that. The metal flapped with a screeching sound freaking her out. Turning to run, Jillian tripped and fell skinning her knees and landing hard on her palms. *What a klutz!* She looked down to see what she'd tripped on and found herself facing the vacant-eyed skull of a horse with yellowed teeth protruding from its bottom jaw. Jumping up, Jillian shuddered. It was then she realized there were bones strewn all across the desert floor. It was creepy and totally gross. Poised to flee, she heard a distinct snort. It sounded like a horse. A living horse.

Putting her revulsion on hold, Jillian hurried to the pile of metal and gently lifted off the top piece. She saw a tangle of brown, filthy forelock. She struggled to lift the second, larger panel. It was four feet across and six feet long, and for a twelve-year-old girl weighing ninety pounds, it was heavy and clumsy to manipulate. Jillian wriggled her arm underneath and hoisted it up while sliding it back.

"Oh, no!"

There, lying on the ground looking like death itself, was a horse. It appeared so fragile and helpless. Every bone was showing; the filthy reddish coat was matted and stuck with burrs, while the mane and tail were packed with dirt. The horse blew from its nostrils making that same rasping sound, and the poor thing tried to lift its head, but it fell back.

"Oh my gosh, you poor, poor thing," cried Jillian. She was amazed that the creature was still alive. She crouched down by the horse's head and reached out a tentative hand to stroke the rough-textured hair on its neck. "They must have forgotten you," she exclaimed, knowing just how that would feel. She saw that the horse was female. "You poor girl. You poor, sweet girl." Jillian rose and looked down the driveway willing the rescuers to come back.

The mare nickered lightly and tried to move to her chest, her thin legs scrambling to find balance. The clatter of metal scared them both, but Jillian reached down and was able to drag off all but one of the remaining metal sheets. Stroking the horse once more, she whispered, "It's okay. You'll be alright." The weak animal managed to fold her forelegs under her chest before she slowly rested her chin in the sand. "Let me get you a drink," Jillian said, thinking out loud. She picked her way out of the pen to the corral where the trough still held a few inches of water. Looking around for something to carry it, she found an old blue plastic bucket with the handle broke half off and a crack in the side. Jillian scooped as much water as the bucket could hold and threaded her way back to the waiting horse.

"Here you go, girl," she said, as she set the bucket on the ground and tipped the front toward her making it easier for the mare to reach. Jillian couldn't help a small self-satisfied smile when the horse sucked loudly on the water. The smile faded as she realized she knew very little about horses. What could she do for her? She was trying to remember the name of the rescue group that was printed on the door of the truck and trailer. Jillian would have to let her grandma know, but that would mean Uncle Aaron would know too, and he would just want to shoot the horse; she was sure of it.

Jillian knew that horses ate grass, oats, and hay. She scanned the area but there was no hay in sight, which didn't surprise her. There were some scraggly weeds growing next to the mobile home. Jillian hesitated, not knowing if they were safe for the horse to eat.

Standing next to the young mare, Jillian knew she had to do something. She thought back to what her uncle had said about their other neighbor, Bill. She hadn't met the man yet, but maybe he would know what to do? She eyed the weeds by the trailer and then looked at the emaciated mare. Jillian was surprised to find the horse looking directly at her and was even more surprised to see the spark of intelligence there. And there was something else, compassion? Was this sick horse feeling sorry for her? It couldn't be. That wouldn't make sense. But she could see something there and she felt compelled to help the starving horse.

"Okay, girl. Here's what I'm going to do. I'm going to leave you here for just a little while. I promise I won't be long," she explained, as she crouched down to stroke the filly on her neck. "I'm going to pick a few of those green weeds for you. I hope they don't make you sick, but I can tell you must be so hungry." Jillian frowned feeling a surge of anger at that young man in the cap who had just left these horses to die. The anger fueled her determination, and she stood up.

The weeds grew in abundance around the shaded side of the mobile home, and Jillian was reaching down into a tall clump of weeds when she froze. She heard a loud rattling sound. Recalling her grandmother's warning, she took a step back. She had never seen a rattlesnake and didn't want to see one now. She took another step backward and there! It moved! The snake slithered in her direction. Jillian was frozen with fear as she watched it gather itself in loops, its eyes fixed on her. The crisscross pattern of black scales down its back was beautiful and terrifying at the same time. It must have been three feet long and was curled up not two feet away from her now, its tail buzzing angrily. An involuntary scream escaped her lips and her eyes widened with fear. She couldn't move! Her legs weren't listening. The snake reared up its head feigning a strike at her.

She felt it before she even heard it. A huge man with sandy hair and a full red beard swung an old shovel at the snake with a whoosh! He simultaneously reached out his thick arm and swept Jillian back and out of the way. His aim was true. The snake, beheaded and helpless, twisted for a few moments in a final dance.

Jillian stared at the dead rattlesnake, then back at the man. He was big, and she was grateful to him for saving her from the snake, but then she felt a twinge of fear. Who was he and what was he doing here?

CHAPTER 3 - Decisions, Decisions

J illian wasn't sure whether she should thank the man for killing the snake and probably saving her life, or run as fast as she could back home. She tensed, poised to flee. The big man turned and looked at her, taking a step backward, as if he could tell she was ready to bolt.

The burly man spoke first, "Hey, young lady. Ya almost got yerself bit there." Eyeing her ivory skin and the bright curls that framed her face. "Ya gotta be real careful in the long grass," he explained. "Those rattlers like ta stay cool in the middle of the day. They're jus' waking up an getting active 'bout this time of year, so ya hafta be extra mindful."

Jillian began to relax as her fear diminished. "I heard it, and I backed up, but it kept coming at me," she said shuddering at the memory.

"They sometimes do that. Oh, an' my name's Bill. Bill Stewart. I live down the hill, on the other side of Allison's place. I bet you're 'er granddaughter. I heard that you was coming ta live here. It must be hard, comin' from Seattle. I went to Seattle once. It was beautiful, but it rains. An' rains. Oh, an I'm sure sorry 'bout your folks. I really am." His blue eyes were filled with compassion.

When Jillian glanced at Bill, she could tell him meant it. "Thanks," she replied, not knowing what to say next.

Then she remembered what she was doing there. She looked at the big man again and realized her stroke of luck. She had been thinking of asking for his help, and here he was. Jillian turned and looked toward where the mare lay hidden behind the pile of metal. "I have a question for you, um, Bill, sir," she began" Do you know anything about horses?"

Bill looked down at her with a surprised expression, his blue eyes twinkling with interest. "Well, yes. I do know some 'bout horses. Not as much as Ole Hank used ta, but I've kept a horse or two in my years," he replied.

"Um, can you keep a secret? I mean, not tell my uncle or grandma? Please?" she said as she stared up at Bill, eyebrows lifted with hope.

"Well, young lady, if you're in some kinda trouble, I can't do nothin' to help ya—," he started.

"No! Nothing like that. It's just," and she looked at the pen where the mare lay waiting, "It is just that Uncle Aaron said they should kill them all and I don't want anything to happen to her!" The intensity of Jillian's concern for the horse surprised even herself.

"Okay, why don'tcha tell me what's goin on, an I'll see what I kin do ta help," Bill replied in a calm voice and a steady smile.

"I think it is better if I show you," answered Jillian, feeling less panic and hoping that she was doing the right thing. "Follow me," she said and turned toward the pen.

When they arrived, the horse looked up at them with huge eyes, and Jillian noticed that her pointed ears were curved toward each other as they pricked forward in anticipation.

"Well, now. What have we got here?" Bill asked the young mare. He crouched down, making himself appear less intimidating. He wore faded jeans that were belted under a belly that was almost as wide as his giant chest. The gentleness he exuded toward the filly seemed in contrast with his burly size, Jillian thought.

"Looks like they missed one, eh?" he asked, assessing the horse.

"I was here watching from the entrance when they were taking away the horses. I didn't see her until they were gone. I mean… I heard her first. I don't know much about horses, and I didn't know what to do, and I am afraid that Uncle Aaron will come and kill her," Jillian rushed on, her words coming out in a jumble. "Can you help her? Can we save her?"

Jillian gave Bill a beseeching look, her eyes wide, lower lip slightly protruding. He looked from the horse to Jillian and said, "Well, we should really call the rescue. They're the ones who're responsible for 'er now." He pulled out his cell phone. "I really think that's what we oughta do, don't ya? If she's too weak to travel, then we'll take care of 'er 'til she is strong enough," he added, giving Jillian hope that maybe, just maybe they could keep her, even for a little while.

As Bill stood up and searched for the number on his cell, Jillian sat next to the horse biting her lip and occasionally stroking the mare on her dirty neck. She looked down at the abandoned animal and felt the weird connection they had made so quickly; it brought tears to her eyes. She knew she was emotional because of her parents, but what she felt with this young horse was the first emotion other than sadness, anger, and grief she had felt since their death. She sensed the filly was the first friend she had made since that horrible day. As her eyes filled with tears, the mare nickered and nosed her hand. Jillian wrapped her arms around the mare's neck. Tears flowed silently and the neglected horse didn't move an inch, allowing the grieving girl to open up. After she was cried out, Jillian felt a small sense of peace. She didn't even notice when Bill walked away, his ear to the phone.

As Bill moved a ways off, Jillian took a minute to examine the mare. She had no idea about her age, but it was clear the horse was almost mature. Her widely spaced eyes, the size of black plums, were full and lustrous. Her muzzle, petite. Jillian once again noted her ears and how they pointed toward each other as the filly looked curiously in her direction. *Her coat looks like red clay.* It was hard to tell the true color of the horse's dirt-filled mane. Jillian thought it a shame that they would probably have to shave it off in order to get rid of the burrs that were tangled in her matted hair.

A wide smile spread over Bill's face as he returned. "Well, it looks like we got a horse ta take care of—fer a while at least," he began, and Jillian jumped up startling the filly, who tried to follow suit. "Whoa girl, easy there," Bill said in a calm voice, and the horse settled back down. "We'll get 'er up soon," he said to Jillian, "but let's clear a path first. We can't leave 'er here on this property. Ole Hank would'na minded, but his kid's a jerk. Oops, sorry," he corrected himself. "I mean, he is not very, um, cooperative. An' we both know that the snakes are out, so this isn't the safest place for 'er."

Jillian experienced a growing tightness of excitement in her belly. "What are we going to do with her? What did the lady from the rescue say?"

"Jennifer, who runs Healin' Horses Rescue, said that with the filly as weak as she is, it'd be safer fer us ta keep 'er 'round here for a coupla weeks 'til she kin be moved safely. So, looks like we're stuck with ya for a bit, girl," he said smiling down at the filly, who appeared to be following the conversation.

Well, it wasn't forever, but at least for the next few weeks Jillian would be able to see the filly every day. She was eager to get her settled. "Where will she live?" she asked with concern, realizing that there might not be an appropriate place to keep the horse at Bill's house, and she certainly couldn't take her home to Grandma's.

"Well, kiddo," he said with a satisfied smile, "I happen ta have two stalls an' a corral at my house. I haven't used 'em in years, but they're empty an she oughta be jus' fine in there. "I think if we clear a good path for 'er, once we get this li'l girl on 'er feet an outta this crappy pen, then she oughta make it ta my house jus' fine. We jus' need ta git a halter on 'er. I don't have one that'd fit 'er but, let's see what we kin find 'round here. Look for a halter or a piece a rope, or a lead line—it looks like a thick dog leash," he explained, noting Jillian's blank expression. They began scouting the area.

Minutes later, Bill found what they needed. "Here, this'll work," he said, holding up a piece of rope. It was about six feet long, soft and pliable, bleached white by the sun. It had a broken clip at one end. "Yup, this is an ole lead rope. This'll jus' work fine," he repeated, and they walked together back to the filly. "Let's clear a good path here, okay? There's so much junk fer 'er ta trip on. Gimme a hand an we'll get 'er outta here."

Jillian pointed out the bits of bone and the skull she'd tripped on. Bill sighed and shook his head moving the skeletal remains carefully out their path. Jillian helped him toss rocks, debris, and pieces of metal in a path that was about five feet wide—room for the mare and Bill to walk side-by-side. Next, in order to give the horse room to stand up, Bill moved the mess of corrugated metal roofing that had collapsed on her, which Jillian had flipped off of the horse when she first arrived. Jillian marveled at how easily Bill picked up the large sheets of metal, and she was grateful this gigantic human was helping her and the horse.

With the garbage out of the way and a rope to control the mare, Jillian felt they were ready to get going. She had faith that if all else failed, Bill could carry the horse to his house. She was intrigued to see what he did with the rope. First, he looped the rope over the filly's nose and crisscrossed it under her chin. Then he brought it up over her head, behind her ears, and slipped the ends through the loop he made under her muzzle. When he pulled it snugly, it looked quite a bit like a halter, and the mare responded immediately splaying her forelegs in front of her.

"Good girl," Bill encouraged her, handing the ends of the rope to Jillian. "Jus' hold onta this an' step back a little when she gits up. I'm gonna give 'er a hand."

With that, Bill stepped to the horse's side and reached his huge arms around her hind end. She scrambled with both front and back legs this time, and with Bill's help, she was on her feet. "Okay now, let's jus' lead 'er slowly outta the pen. She's probably gonna be a lil' wobbly, so I'll stay back here, an' you take the lead. Jus' walk slowly an' I'm sure she'll follow."

Uncertain about leading the horse, Jillian took a tentative step forward, and the filly followed with a staggery step of her own. One, two, three slow steps and she looked at the young horse. She saw a determined light in the horse's otherwise dull appearance and it gave her a warm feeling of hope. It strengthened her resolve to nurse the resilient mare back to health.

The walk from Hank's place to Bill's took about fifteen minutes. The filly started and stopped a few times, but with gentle encouragement from Jillian, and a little muscle from Bill, they made it down the hill and turned left onto Bill's road. All the roads were dirt and there were no cars, making the trip uneventful.

"Here we go," said Bill as they walked down his driveway, which was marked by a giant Saguaro and an artful collection of desert stone. Jillian was shocked when she saw

Bill's house. Well, not so much the house, which was typical Southwestern style; it was the landscaping around the house that gave Jillian pause. "Yeah, well, I kinda like ta garden a bit," Bill said with a shy smile.

Flowers and plants of all colors surrounded the home. There was a grass lawn. Grass! She hadn't seen a lawn this big and well-manicured anywhere since she'd arrived in Phoenix, except at the park in Anthem. This was a real lawn, thick and green: the kind that you want to run on with your bare feet, and play on with your dog, or lie on your back and watch the clouds. All around the lawn's edges, up the walkway to the front door, and in pots around the patio, were flowers and plants in a mind-blowing abundance of green, pink, white, and yellow. Purple wisteria hung over the metal archway that covered the entry gate to the front yard. Bright red bougainvillea graced the short wall around the yard, and a mighty Saguaro cactus stood tall and proud next to the house guarding it against intruders. Poppies, daisies, and flowers of all types added to the riot of color.

Jillian felt herself smile, the kind of smile that starts deep on the inside and can't help but burst out. The combination of emotion, stress, loss, and then this amazing scene of color and life, filled her with a lightness that she hadn't felt in ages.

"Wow. This place is beautiful! Really beautiful, Bill."

Bill shook his head in embarrassment, and she thought she saw a little blush on his cheeks. The juxtaposition of Bill's physical demeanor to the creative, kind side he possessed struck her, and she followed up. "You really shouldn't be embarrassed. You have a lot of talent. I didn't think anyone could ever keep this much stuff alive in the desert!"

Bill brushed off the compliment, saying, "Here, the corral's this way," and he urged the mare onward, toward the side of the house where Jillian could see a metal roof surrounded with fencing. They got the horse in the corral with no problem and Bill filled up a water bucket for her, which she drank greedily. "I don't have any hay here, so I'm gonna run ta the feed store an' get some. Are ya okay staying here alone with 'er while I'm gone?" he asked.

"If I can take off my shoes and walk on your lawn, I'll stay," Jillian replied with a grin.

"Ha! Course ya kin! You kin even pick some of it fer the filly. There's a spot jus' behind the house on this side of the backyard where I haven't mowed yet. An' don't worry 'bout snakes, I checked it before I left an' I'll double-check, but it was rattler-free the last time I looked." After a quick snake-check, Bill got into his truck and took off leaving Jillian and the filly alone.

This time, Jillian didn't feel lonely at all. She went through the corral gate and onto the front lawn. She bent down to take off her shoes but changed her mind. Instead, she turned and walked into the backyard. Reaching the patch of unmowed lawn, she began picking the mid-length grass. The filly pricked her ears and nickered, tossing her head with impatience. Jillian looked up at her. "I'm hurrying!" she said, shaking her head with an indulgent grin and picking a few more handfuls before taking it back to the horse. "I guess you like that, huh?" The little mare gobbled up the grass she had brought. "Don't worry, I'll get you some more," she chuckled and went back for another batch.

Jillian still hadn't stopped to take off her shoes and enjoy the lawn when Bill returned thirty minutes later. He sat in his car and smiled as he watched the girl feeding grass to the grateful horse, and he felt a moment of peace himself. He missed his wife. He missed having her company. He missed talking to her and sharing his ideas. Bill thought Clara would have liked this girl. She had spunk, much like his Clara. He sighed, smiled. He would call Allison and make sure he got permission for the girl to visit. He didn't have to mention the horse. At least not right away.

"Did you see her eating the grass? She really likes it!" Jillian called out as Bill carried the big bale of hay to the little shed next to corral.

"I bet she does," he replied with a grin. "I think she'll like this hay too, an' it's a far bit easier ta feed than pickin' a whole buncha grass," he added. "We hafta be real careful how much we feed 'er, an what she eats at first. She kin have hay an' water, but no grain or anything else fer the first coupla weeks."

"But she's starving. Why can't we just give her a whole bunch of hay?" asked Jillian.

"Well, 'er body's not used ta eatin' much so we hafta go slow, 'specially in the beginnin'. If she were ta eat too much, she could get real sick," Bill explained.

"Really? Well, I don't want that to happen. How do we know when she can safely eat more food?" she asked, curious to understand how to help the little mare get stronger and healthy.

"Well, the rescue recommended that we feed 'er this alfalfa at first. She kin have a quarter flake now, then I'll give 'er some more in an hour or two. She can eat lil' bits at a time 'til 'er belly's ready fer a full meal." Bill went on. "The rescue'll have the vet come out an' take a look at 'er too. When we get the okay, we'll start givin' 'er more, but even wormin' medicine could hurt 'er in the shape she's in right now."

Bill handed Jillian a portion of hay that he called a "flake" which he'd torn it into quarters. Jillian took the small bundle and carried it over to the horse putting it in the feeder that hung off the rail. The young mare hungrily started munching; the slim girl and the giant man stood in silence listening to her eat.

The grinding sound of her teeth and the smell of the green alfalfa were soothing. It was not exactly a miracle or anything, but Jillian felt her life had made a shift in a good direction.

Horse Thoughts

So much fear. So much hunger and thirst! Time cannot be told. Little or nothing to eat for long. Dust. Sand. Heat. No protection. Just the herd. And peril.

Hazy memories. First start small. Our Two-Legger-with-Smoke that burns my nostrils, He feeds. He waters. He strokes. There is love. And play. Until he begins to forget.

Thin Two-Legger comes sometimes when Two-Legger-with-Smoke stops. He brings sour hay. Not much. Never enough. Never joyful.

Then nothing. Water from the sky only. Heat. Dry and parched. Always. Gnawing pangs, my shadows. Smaller: all the herd. Time passes. Strength bolts. Then death. And again. And again. The Eaters come and take the dead. Eaters small and large. Winged. Crawling. Stalking. Slithering. Threatening. Circling. The herd made small. Weak. Eaters are close. I pin my ears flat. Bare my teeth, and show my sharp hooves. The Eaters are wary.

Fear rides us all. Day and night and day again. Flaps. Screeches of metal. Wind rises. Flashes of light. Death is close. No safety. No rest. No play. I give up. Lie down. Herd guards, waiting.

Sudden pain! Crashing! Darkness! No flight. No fight. Almost peace. Sleep.

Then the two-leggers take my herd. Silence. Fear. Acceptance. I am ready.

But, the Small One comes. She brings her sadness. Dark-scented waves, oozing. Loneliness flares. At first, overwhelming—loneliness and grief. It shrouds the Small One in a grey-blue haze. I know the same haze. Hidden there in darkness: hearing, smelling, tasting my herd depart. My mother's defiant cries. Then alone. I cannot rise. I despair. Yellow fear and pain. Yet, The Small One knows. She feels it. She shares it with me. She saves me.

Oh, the rich scent of green! I lip leafy flakes, grinding life. The two-leggers stand watching. Staring. I raise my head, ears pricked toward them. Need I flee? I feel no bad intent.

The Small One sends warmth. A small happiness. Now is food. And water. And trust? Joy is close.

CHAPTER 4 – A New Day

The alarm buzzed at 6:30, but Jillian was already lying awake in bed thinking about the first day of school and wondering what time she would be getting home so she could see the filly. She had returned from Bill's yesterday afternoon, and much to her grandma's surprise, offered to set the table and help start dinner.

Allison was curious to know why the girl appeared to be so happy, but she didn't want to pry and spoil the mood, so she worked alongside Jillian cleaning up the kitchen in silence for a while.

"How was your day?" she asked. "Did you see Hank's horses? I hope they made it to safety. Were they all okay?"

Jillian answered, trying to decide if she should tell her grandma about the mare she found. "Um, yeah, I saw them. It was sad. They were skinny, but they're all safe now," she added. She couldn't bring herself to say anything more to her grandmother about it yet. But she did need to tell her about seeing Bill. She didn't want her grandma to worry about her.

"Oh, and I met our neighbor Bill."

"Well, dear, that's good. He's a very nice man. He's lived here for as long as I have. His wife Clara passed away a few years back. It was tough on him like it was tough on me when I lost Sam." Her eyes were far away. "Of course, it's nothing like losing your parents," she added.

"Is it okay if I visit his garden sometimes and help him?" Jillian asked.

"What a kind thing to offer, Jillian! Of course, you can. Just let me know when you visit him, okay?"

"Sure, Grandma. And thanks. I might drop by to help him tomorrow. I'd better get ready for school. Argh!" She rolled her eyes. Her grandma smiled at her.

"School won't be that bad," she chided. "At least you'll meet some girls your own age."

Last night, Jillian had prepared what she was going to wear on her first day: grey leggings, a long blue t-shirt, her Converse sneakers, and her Mariner's ball cap. She didn't know what girls wore in Arizona; she hoped she would fit in. She couldn't remember ever being the "new girl" in school. She had been friends with Janet since they were practically born, and she'd known all the girls at the Washington middle school from the time they were in daycare and preschool.

Jillian was nervous about the day, and she still couldn't believe her grandma was making her go for just two weeks! That was totally stupid. She had to waste her time at the end of the school year, when she knew no one and nothing at all about what they were studying. Would she have to take their final exams? Was she expected to know everything they had taught?

Since her parents passing, Jillian had attended some school, but between the funeral, packing, and traveling to Arizona, she hadn't even looked at a school book in over a month. But Grandma Allison said she would at least meet some kids. Two days ago, meeting new kids at school was both exciting and scary. Now, she'd rather spend time with the horse next door.

The thought spurred her into action, out of bed and into the shower. Bill had promised she could help brush the mare this morning before she left for school. She checked herself in the bathroom mirror. She'd battled her shoulder-length red curls and somehow corralled them into a ponytail that peeked out under the brim of the ball cap she wore backward. Her light blue eyes seemed huge in her face, and they made her look younger than her twelve years. She groaned when she noticed her freckles seemed to be larger and darker than usual. Jillian rolled her eyes at her reflection, took a deep breath, and flipped off the light.

Allison was again surprised at her granddaughter's perky attitude at breakfast. For the last few weeks, breakfast had been a silent affair, but today Jillian was almost chatty.

Grandma Allison had packed a lunch for Jillian that was so big, the brown paper bag wouldn't come anywhere near closing. The girl ate her cereal, thanked her grandmother, put her oversized lunch in her backpack, and headed out the door.

"The bus doesn't come for twenty minutes!" called Grandma Allison, but Jillian just waved and trotted out the drive. She justified not mentioning that she was going to Bill's house before school by the comment she'd made about him last night.

Bill was in his house when Jillian arrived, so she went straight to the corral where the mare was munching hay. She was pleased to hear a nicker.

"It's so good to see you eating, big girl! You look better already," she crooned taking a step backward and looking at the horse. Her coat was coarse and rough, and you could see her ribs and hipbones, but her eyes were bright and she seemed steadier on her feet. Jillian smiled at the transformation between the happily eating animal and the desperate horse of less than a day ago.

Bill showed up moments later with a few grooming tools. "I don't want ya ta get all dirty before ya go ta school, so why not jus' help me a little with 'er mane. When ya get home this afternoon, I'll have all the burrs an' knots out, an' we can give 'er a bath. What do you think?" he asked, smiling and handing her a metal comb with a wooden handle. "Jus' start combing 'er mane in sections, workin' from the bottom to the top. An' here, use this," he said, handing her a white bottle that read 'Cowboy Magic.' "Ya jus' squirt the gel in yer hand an' massage it onto 'er mane. It's a detangler, so when ya comb 'er mane, it makes it a little easier ta work the knots an' stickers out."

Jillian squirted some of the coconut scented goo on her hands and rubbed them together and then worked it into the filly's mane starting at the base of her neck. It wasn't easy. Combing out the prickers was painful work. Jillian was pleased that despite her tugging and teasing out knots, the mare seemed to be relaxed and enjoying the attention. Jillian wasn't even a quarter of the way done when Bill stopped her telling her it was time to catch the bus

"I'll see you this afternoon!" she proclaimed brightly, as she washed off her scratched hands in the hose and headed to the bus stop.

Bill smiled with a sense of peace he hadn't felt in a long time. Since Clara died, he had been lonely. This little girl and her destitute horse filled a gap he hadn't realized was there, and it made him wonder about the timing of things that happen in life. It sure felt to him like there was someone or something with a plan that he just didn't understand.

There were only a few kids on the bus when Jillian climbed on board. The bus driver was a woman with dark messy hair and sunglasses who looked like she had just woken up. "Howdy. You must be new. I'm Janice, and I'll be driving you for the next couple weeks. Don't be late. I don't wait. Welcome to New River." And with that, she nodded and closed the door.

Without waiting for Jillian to sit down, Janice stepped on the gas, sending the bus roaring down the hill. Jillian stumbled into the seat behind the driver. She felt her stomach tighten with anticipation of her first day of school.

Jillian went straight to the office that Grandma had taken her to last week when she registered. She let them know who she was and seconds later heard an announcement: "Whitney Briggs to the front office for escort! Whitney Briggs!"

Almost ten minutes later, and after the second bell had rung, Whitney Briggs strolled into the office. Jillian could tell the second she saw the girl as she came around the corner— still snickering at some joke her friend had just told —that they were not going to get along. There wasn't anything specific about the blonde girl that made her feel that way, but she could tell they were very, very different.

Whitney was what Jillian thought of as a "fashionista female." As she moseyed into the office, her mid-thigh length, eggplant-colored skirt with pleats all around and a wide tight waistband showed off a tiny waist and long, tanned legs. She wore a tight top with a geometric dark brown and white pattern that didn't quite meet the top of her skirt. Her hair, long and flaxen, hung in perfect slow curls, and she wore a hint of makeup.

By comparison, Jillian's simple blue t-shirt and grey leggings were plain and unremarkable; she struggled not to feel like a frump.

"Oh, you must be Jillian, the new girl," exclaimed Whitney with fake enthusiasm. She eyed Jillian's outfit, her red hair, and light complexion with a dismissive look.

"Yup. That's me," replied Jillian, with equally-feigned eagerness, standing up to follow Whitney out into the hallway.

When they were a few paces down the hall from the office, Whitney turned, putting her hands on her hips and offered Jillian an exasperated look, saying, "Well, I guess you have the same classes as me, and I'm on a silly restriction. So as some sort of 'payback,' I'm supposed to show you around. Just stay out of my way and follow me." She gave Jillian another once over and turned, stalking off down the hall, leaving Jillian with no doubt as to her undesired company.

Humiliated, Jillian followed Whitney to English, their first class. And because they were late, they attracted notice when they entered. Whitney took full advantage of the attention. She shook her blonde hair and smiled at her friends as she pranced off to her seat. Jillian followed, feeling strange and awkward. She found a desk at the back of the room and slunk down into the chair wishing she could just sink into the floor and disappear.

"You must be the new student, um, Jillian. Is that right?" The teacher smiled at her.

"Yes, I'm Jillian Sullivan," she managed to reply, already flushed with embarrassment.

"Class, let's all welcome Jillian," her teacher urged. A smattering of half-hearted applause followed and then class began.

To her surprise, the course work wasn't so different from what she had been learning in Seattle. She tried to pay attention to the teacher and take notes, ignoring the sideways glances from the other students. When the bell rang, she gathered her papers and took her time getting organized waiting for most of the other kids to leave.

"Come on!" insisted Whitney, beckoning with a wave of her hand. "You don't want to make us late to the next class too, do you?"

Their next class was history with Mr. Gunther. It was a repeat of English in that Jillian spent the class either watching the teacher write on the board or staring at her history book. Sitting in front of her was an exotic-looking girl with creamy, light brown skin, and long straight black hair, who, like Jillian, was wearing a backward ball cap. She smiled when Jillian walked to her seat. It was the first real smile she had received, and Jillian flashed her a quick grin. History finally ended. She had a study period next.

When Whitney flounced by beckoning Jillian with a forefinger, the girl who had been sitting in front of her turned to Jillian. "Hi, my name's Lila. I'm in the same study period as you and Whitney," she said, with a frown in the direction of the door where Whitney and her flock of friends were whispering and giggling. "Do you want to me to show you the way?" she asked.

Jillian was surprised, but grateful. "Yes! I mean, er, yes, please." She sprang to her feet failing to hide her enthusiasm at ditching Whitney and her air-headed friends. Lila grinned.

"Looks like I'll take over showing her to study hall," Lila said, with a dismissive wave to Whitney as they walked past the trio of girls waiting in the hall. Lila and Jillian looked at each other as they walked away and burst out laughing.

"Did you see the look on her face?," exclaimed Jillian. "It was awesome. Thanks so much for rescuing me. I don't know that girl very well, but I don't like her at all."

"She is one of those stupid, supposedly 'popular girls,' and she does her best to try to feel superior. Just ignore her and try not to tick her off too much," added Lila. "She's got a dumb group of girls, plus some boys who think she's cool. But, let's not talk about her. What about you?" she asked, as they were walking to study hall. "Obviously you're new here," she said, using her hands as she talked. "When did you move here, and how come you're here for the last two weeks? That seems nuts!"

"Tell me about it!" said Jillian. "I did not want to come to school, but my grandmother said I had to. I think it's dumb."

"Oh, you live with your grandma? That's cool," Lila responded

"Well, I do now." Jillian started and then she stopped in the hall, turning to her rescuer, who looked at her curiously. "My parents were killed in a car crash a couple of months ago," she continued in a soft voice dropping her gaze to the hallway floor.

"Oh, no! I'm so sorry." Lila's hand flew to cover her mouth. "That must be really hard."

"No, it's okay. I mean, no, it's not okay. Nothing is okay anymore, well almost nothing," Jillian replied, thinking of the horse. She turned and continued down the hall, both of them silent. Jillian didn't want pity, but it felt good to tell someone. She hoped that Lila wouldn't go blabbing to other kids about it.

Almost as if she read Jillian's mind, Lila said, "I won't tell anyone. It must be really hard. And I'm sorry." She reached out and put her hand on Jillian's shoulder. "Here we are at study hall. Then we can have lunch, and you can meet my best friend," Lila went on in a forced-happy voice.

Study hall flew by. Both girls had lots of preparation for the exams Jillian learned she would have to take. Jillian was grateful to have someone to ask questions when she got stuck. It seemed like they had just walked into class when they were walking right out again.

The lunchroom was loud, and the tables were filling up. To the left stood the lunch buffet, and they headed to the line. Jillian had her gigantic lunch but joined Lila as she waited in line. She asked Lila what she did for fun after school.

"I love to bake and cook stuff. See, my mom has a Thai food restaurant. I'm half Thai and half white, or whatever. I get to help in the restaurant sometimes, but mostly while Mom is at work, I cook for the family at home, or I make cookies or cakes with my friends. Do you like to cook?" she asked Jillian.

"Um, well, I don't know how to cook much. I mean, I guess I can make eggs and breakfast stuff. My mom loved to cook, and she spent hours in the kitchen humming while she cooked us all kinds of amazing meals." Jillian frowned at the end of the sentence.

Lila knitted her brows in concern. "You okay?" she asked.

"Yeah, I'm okay." Jillian blinked hard and shook her head. "I'm fine. No, I haven't done too much cooking, but I like eating, and I love chocolate chip cookies. Can you make chocolate chips?" she asked.

"Can I make chocolate chip cookies she wonders?" Lila gave a smug smile. "I can make dark chocolate chip cookies with or without macadamia nuts or pecans or almonds. I can make white chocolate chip cookies or milk chocolate chip cookies. I can make them gluten free if you want. Or sugar free, which is kinda gross. I can make them crunchy or chewy or out of organic ingredients. You name it, I can make that cookie." Lila looked at Jillian with a silly face and a grin. They both burst out laughing and were giggling when a tall girl with long dark blonde hair approached them.

"Hey, Lila!" She turned to Jillian. "Hi, I'm Aubrey. You must be the new girl that Whitney was dragging around earlier.

Sorry about that. She is... well, let's just say she is not a very nice person. And you must be a nice person if Lila is hanging out with you," she added with a quick smile at Lila.

Jillian was happy to meet someone else who seemed nice. The two girls got their trays, and they found an open table that was out of the main flow of kids. Aubrey and Lila sat facing Jillian.

"Aubrey lives not very far from me, and she is the smartest girl in seventh grade," Lila announced, nodding proudly at her friend. Aubrey responded by pushing Lila on the shoulder and blushing. "She is modest, but it's true. Brilliant. And also great to have as a friend when you need to study," Lila grinned. "She lives off Lazy G Road. Don't you live around there?" she asked Jillian.

"I think so. I mean, that sounds familiar. I haven't paid too much attention to the names of roads. I've only been here, like, three weeks. I took the bus to school, and I think it might have seen the name." Jillian felt silly not even knowing where she lived.

Aubrey came to the rescue. "Oh, yes, you live close to me. We take the same bus. I saw you this morning when you got on. You kinda got tossed behind the driver. You have to be ready with Janice; she steps on the gas as soon as the door is closed. And when she says, 'Don't be late, I don't wait,' you better believe her!" Aubrey grinned at Jillian, who smiled and nodded. "I just live down the hill and up that awful steep, bumpy road. That's the one called Lazy G. You and I are neighbors," she concluded. Her blue eyes were smiling, and Jillian sensed that she was honestly happy about it.

A surge of gratitude for their budding friendship swept over Jillian as she looked across the table at the girls. They were so different: Lila was lithe with Asian features, dark hair, flashing eyes, and bubbling enthusiasm. Aubrey was tall, quiet, thoughtful, and serene with soft blondish-brown hair that she kept out of her face with a clip. Jillian mused that she added the third and final quirky element to their trio with her curly red hair and masses of freckles.

As if reading her mind, Lila said, "We are kinda different from each other, aren't we? It's funny how sometimes the friends you like best are the ones who are the most different from you. At least that's the case with me and Aubs. Now, with your curly red hair and white skin and freckles, you look totally different than both of us. I think you'll fit nicely into our misfit group!" She giggled.

Lunch ended far too soon, and the girls set off for afternoon classes. Jillian learned either Lila or Aubrey were in all her afternoon classes. She was glad not to have to spend any more time following Whitney. She wasn't used to being "new." The acceptance she felt from Aubrey and Lila helped her through that first day. As Jillian greeted Janice and settled next to Aubrey for the ride home, she didn't feel nearly as awkward as she had when she walked off the same bus just hours earlier.

CHAPTER 5 – Jealousy

The bus ride home flew by. Aubrey kept asking questions, and they talked and laughed the whole way home. Jillian was basking in the feeling of new friendship when she realized she hadn't thought of her parents since lunchtime. Her eyes furrowed, but Aubrey brought her out of her reverie, asking, "Were your classes here tough compared to Washington?"

"Some were harder and a couple were easier. The coursework is similar to what I'm used to. But math is like, ugh! I'm not so great in Social Studies either. What about you? Do you take special smart-kid classes?" Jillian asked, smiling.

"Well, I do take 'special smart-kid classes' in English, math, and science." Aubrey grinned back. "But I'm still in 'regular-kid classes' for the rest."

"Whoops, this is my stop, I'll see you tomorrow." Jillian stood up, and Aubrey gave her a quick wave goodbye. She walked off the bus feeling good.

Grandma Allison was in the kitchen when Jillian announced her arrival with the banging of the front door screen.

"Hi, Jillian. How was your first day?" she asked.
"Not too bad for a first day, Grandma. Thanks for asking." Jillian headed to her room to change.

Allison's amused gaze followed the girl down the hall. She hoped Jillian was being honest. She worried about her granddaughter and felt helpless to communicate with her in a meaningful way. Allison herself was still grieving the loss of her daughter. She wished she had gone to the funeral, even though she'd been sick. She wished she had visited her daughter more often. Regret pricked and tears swam as she remembered her daughter at Jillian's age.

Allison and Sam had married young, but she was not able to conceive for many years. She was twenty-six when she had Janie, Jillian's mother. It was almost twelve years later when she and her husband were surprised when Allison got pregnant with Aaron. With so many years between brother and sister, her children were not close, and Janie left for college at seventeen when Aaron was only five.

Janie had always been a bright girl. She was athletic and played competitive soccer. She wanted to study business in college and received a partial soccer scholarship at Arizona State University. After she moved to school, she rarely came home. She was busy with her own life; Allison understood that. Janie's sporadic visits brought a brightness to the house that she missed. Her self-confidence and earnest need to learn delighted Allison—what a contrast to Aaron's petulant behavior.

Allison knew Aaron had resented his older sister. She had enjoyed years of life with both parents, and their father lavished his affection on his daughter. Sam died of cancer when Aaron was four, just a year before Janie left for school; all of a sudden it was just Aaron and Allison. She knew it had been difficult for him to grow up without a father. She had worked so many hours at the Anthem Post Office just to pay the mortgage and keep food on the table that she missed a lot of his youth. Allison feared she hadn't been there enough for him.

Already a troubled child, Aaron began picking fights and bullying younger kids when he was almost ten. In high school, he cut classes and would disappear for an entire day coming home late at night. That's when the constant arguing began. Oh, she'd hated to argue! Aaron disappeared for a month when he was fifteen. It took five frantic days for him to call her and three more weeks for him to return. Then, at seventeen, he said goodbye and traveled to the South with a friend. It was hard not to feel that she'd failed him.

When Aaron came home four years ago, Allison didn't think he would stay for long, but he'd surprised her and stuck around. They'd had a boarder, Johnny, who had rented the room Jillian now occupied. Johnny's rent paid the utility bills. Aaron brought in sporadic money, but he was always finding jobs that didn't agree with him and then moving on to the next one. He never stayed long enough at any job to advance or be promoted.

Allison sighed thinking about her son. She wished she knew what to say or do to motivate him to make something of himself. She was nearing seventy, and for goodness sake, Aaron was almost thirty years old. It was time for him to get his act together and start making his own way in life with some focus and a steady job.

At that moment, Aaron was pushing out the swinging doors of the Roadrunner Bar & Grill just a few miles away. It had been a rough day. He'd been working for a contractor who had him doing the stupidest jobs. "Hurry up! Come on man, can't you work faster?" was all he'd heard all morning. By lunch Aaron had had enough and walked off the job site. He was definitely worth more than fourteen bucks an hour. Feeling justified he headed to the Roadrunner for a beer or two.

Aaron was well-known to the staff at the neighborhood restaurant. As long as he didn't get too drunk, they put up with him complaining about one thing or another.

Getting into his crappy Toyota about an hour later, Aaron considered maybe he had one too many beers, but it was a short drive home.

An idiot in front of him drove right at the speed limit all the way to his turnoff. He crept along behind the car flashing his headlights. He rolled down his window and hollered, "Jeez, you old geezer, pull over if you can't drive!" But he was forced to maintain the speed limit for the next half mile until he turned off the road and pulled up in front of a row of locked mailboxes.

Aaron turned off the car and got out fumbling for his mailbox key. He was the only one who got the mail. His mother didn't drive, and she wasn't going to walk down and back up the hill to get it. He secretly relished being the first to find any interesting mail, and he had used his advantage to hide several speeding tickets and a number of bills for items she had no idea he'd purchased. Aaron loved his mom, but she was naïve, and while he never thought of it as stealing from her, he took advantage of his mother without hesitation. He felt it was his right. If he'd learned anything from his days on the road, it was that you gotta take care of number one.

The mailbox held mostly grocery ads and real estate postcards, but there was one envelope addressed to his mother from "Steiner & Sons, PLLC," with a Seattle, Washington return address. Aaron got back into his car and sat there thinking. Curious to know what was in the letter, he guessed it had something to do with Janie's estate. Holding the envelope up to the sun didn't help. It was too full of paper. Flipping the envelope over and looking at the seal, Aaron tested it with his finger, but the seal was tight. Considering his options, Aaron decided to open the envelope and tell his mother that it was an accident. Defense resolved, he slid open the flap and emptied the letter onto his lap.

There was something inside it. A check for five thousand dollars! He smoothed the letter and read:

Greetings Mrs. Parker,

*I trust this letter finds you and young Jillian in good health.
Please accept my personal sympathies. Your daughter and her husband
were good friends. They are greatly missed.*

*As you are aware, Mr. and Mrs. Sullivan hired our firm to
manage their estate, and I am enclosing probate documents that outline
their wishes for the distribution of their assets. Some of the Sullivan's hard
assets, including their primary home in Woodinville, Washington, are still
to be sold.*

*You will find a detailed description in the probate paperwork,
however, there are a few highlights that need your attention immediately.*

Aaron drew a deep breath. His sister had assets? He
read on with growing excitement.

*Mr. and Mrs. John and Jane Sullivan left the whole of their
estate to their daughter and minor child, Jillian Annette Sullivan. The
estate is to be held in a trust for Jillian until she reaches the age of twenty-
one, after which she has full access to manage her own trust account. As
her legal guardian, you are charged with overseeing her estate until Jillian's
twenty-first birthday. It was their wish that Jillian receive a monthly
stipend of two thousand dollars ($2,000) of which 20 percent ($400) is to
be provided to Jillian each month to use as she chooses, and the balance of
the stipend to be spent on her care and comfort.*

*In the interest of Jillian's care and your own, the Sullivans have
provided funds to pay off the mortgage on your property in New River,
Arizona, ensuring that Jillian will always have a family home. The funds
have been transferred to your mortgage lender, and they will be sending you
a copy of your clear title and deed of trust soon.*

*Please complete the attached form providing banking information
for monthly deposit of the trust funds. You will receive a follow-up phone
call from our office within the week to confirm additional details. You will
also receive a packet of information about the investments Jillian now owns*

and the additional assets that are involved in her trust. As her legal guardian, all account statements will be sent to your attention.

Enclosed is a check for five thousand dollars ($5,000) to cover Jillian's expenses until the automatic deposit is set up with your bank. It is our pleasure to serve Miss. Sullivan and yourself.

With sincere regards,
William J. Steiner Esq.

Aaron let out the breath he had been holding. This changed things. At first, he wondered if he could get his hands on some of that five grand. His second thought was now he didn't have to worry about work. He just had to placate his mom and keep the kid out of his business, and he could pretty much do whatever he wanted. Dang! He wanted to head back to the Roadrunner and share his good news, but he decided it was more important to get his mother to fill out the bank paperwork so they could have a monthly income.

"Hey Mom, I got the mail," called Aaron as he walked in the back door, letting the screen slam behind him. Allison was in the kitchen starting supper.

"I'll get to it after dinner dear, she answered absently, searching for a can opener. "Oh, and please don't slam the door. You know how that irritates me," she added.

"I think you want to see this. I opened it by mistake, but, um, it's about Jillian or for you, I guess," he replied.

Allison focused on the letter he handed her and almost dropped the check as she unfolded the sheets. She glanced at Aaron sharply, knowing his opening of the letter was no mistake. "I will take care of it, dear," she responded, folding the letter and check back up and putting them both in her purse.

"Don't forget about it now, Ma. This is great for us. I mean for Jillian and for you. No more mortgage payments.

That's pretty awesome! We won't have to work nearly as hard. Do you know how much they had in assets?" All the questions ran together, and she was about to tell him to let it go when Jillian walked in.

"Grandma, I'm heading out to take a little walk and get some fresh air before dinner. I might stop by Bill's house to see if he needs help. I love his garden." Jillian passed through the kitchen ignoring the mail and unaware of the tension between her uncle and her grandmother.

"Be back by 5:30, please, and watch out for snakes," Allison responded.

"Okay, Grandma. See you then. Thanks!"
Jillian seemed in good spirits, and it warmed Allison's heart. Her eyes flicked toward Aaron. She saw the self-satisfied smile on his face, and she had a gut feeling the most dangerous snake to Jillian might just be Aaron himself.

CHAPTER 6 – What's A Jibbah?

Jillian skipped to Bill's house, looking forward to giving the filly a bath. She had been thinking about names and wanted to ask Bill if he had any good ideas. She stopped short, however, as she turned down his driveway and saw the white truck that belonged to the rescue she'd seen at Old Hank's yesterday. Jillian slowed and trudged down the driveway with her heart in her throat. Had the rescue lady come to take the horse away? Was the mare sick? Did Bill think it was a mistake to try to take care of her? The joy she'd felt as she'd left home fled, and her stomach felt an empty tension.

Bill and the woman from the rescue were standing in front of the mare talking. The horse was looking curiously at them; when she saw Jillian, she let out a little nicker. The two adults turned to see Jillian approach.

"Hi, Jillian. I want ya ta meet Jennifer Conner," called Bill. "Jennifer runs the Healin' Horses rescue that picked up all the horses yesterday. Well, almost all the horses," he said, with a wink and a grin.

"Hello, Jillian," greeted Jennifer, tucking her dark blonde hair behind her ear and extending a slender hand. "I want to thank you so much for finding this girl. We were sure we had checked everywhere, but I guess not quite everywhere," she continued with a smile. "Bill tells me that you two have taken quite a shine to each other. I think that's awesome. I brought over a few things she might need and wanted to talk to you about helping us rehab her."

Despite Jillian's fears, it seemed Jennifer wasn't here to take the filly away but to teach her how to provide better care. She let out a breath she had no idea she was holding. Her eyes grew wide with excitement as she began asking questions, one rolling right into the other.

"Do you know what kind of horse she is? How much are we supposed to feed her? What is the best thing for her to eat? She is so skinny; can she get hurt easily? I mean, is she delicate? How old is she, do you know? Will she grow bigger? When can you ride horses? Do I need to get her a new leash? We used an old rope to get her here." Jillian couldn't stop talking and both Bill and Jennifer were grinning.

"Okay, young lady. Jus' hang on a sec an' Jennifer will tell us what we need ta do. She knows 'er stuff. She's really helped Healin' Horses, gettin' volunteers and keepin' the shelter runnin' smooth. They're adoptin' out more horses than ever. She's gonna explain everything."

The young mare edged closer to the three as they were talking and started nodding her head at Jillian. They all laughed. "Looks like she has something to say too, doesn't she?" remarked Jennifer. "You would be surprised at how well horses can learn to communicate with people."

"I think I know what you mean a little bit already," responded Jillian. "Yesterday when we were helping her, I could tell she was scared and thirsty and hungry, but I could also tell that she trusted me. It was really a cool feeling. Is that what you mean?" she asked, looking up at Jennifer while she stroked the filly's forehead and straightened her forelock.

"Yup. That's a part of it. You must have a strong sense of empathy. Horses pick up on people who are sensitive. You'll find that the longer you work with a horse, the deeper your level of understanding can go. Not like you can talk to each other in words, but you can understand what they need, and they understand what you want, sometimes even before you know it."

"I didn't know horses could do that!" Jillian declared, looking the filly in her eyes. "She is smart though, I can tell. Do you know what kind of horse she is? Bill thought that Old Hank kept Arabian horses, but he wasn't sure. I think she's beautiful." Seeming to understand, the little horse began nodding her head again as if in complete agreement. The air rang with their laughter.

"Well, from what I was able to determine, Bill is right. The whole bunch are Arabians. Hank used to breed some impressive horses in his heyday, and while we don't have pedigrees for many of them, including this one here, I'm quite sure they are well-bred," Jennifer explained, tucking her hair behind her ears, her wide grey-blue eyes fringed with full lashes.

When Jillian had first seen Jennifer yesterday at Hank's house, she thought that Jennifer was all business, and she'd been a little intimidated. The Jennifer of yesterday looked tough confronting Hank's son, her uniform of khakis and Healing Horses polo shirt adding authority. Today's Jennifer was dressed in skinny jeans with ankle-high polished boots and a light blue top with cap sleeves that fluttered when she moved. She carried an air of polish about her. She was confident and it showed, but Jillian was beginning to see another side of Jennifer. It was her teaching side, her fun side.

"Why is a pedigree important?" she asked Jennifer, interested to learn more.

"Do you know anything about genetics?" responded Jennifer.

Jillian nodded. "Is that like DNA and chromosomes and stuff like that?"

"Exactly. Your genetics determine the type of inherited characteristics you'll receive from your parents," she explained. "Like when you go to a family reunion and notice your cousins look somewhat like you, or you and your brothers and sisters share some of the same traits but not all of them. It works the same in horses. That's why you can breed the same two horses and get different looking siblings, but they will usually share some traits in common. Some horses have very strong inheritable traits in their pedigrees, and other lineages don't carry qualities that are as strong."

Jillian asked, "How do you know if a horse is going to pass on those qualities to their babies?"

"That is the big mystery of breeding horses. Or any animal, really. The horse's pedigree is its family tree. It will tell you what your horse's traits can or might be. People study pedigrees in-depth so that they can learn which bloodlines carry the particular traits they would like to promote and how to minimize the negative traits of their mare by breeding to a stallion with a heritage that is strong where she is weak or vice versa. Foals get their characteristics from both parents, so it is important for breeders to know traits each bloodline produces."

Jillian had never thought about how horse breeders decided which horse to breed to which. It made sense to look at the horses in the pedigree to understand how a baby could be bred to strengthen important traits.

"Also," Jennifer continued, "if you want to show a horse in a recognized Arabian horse show, it has to be registered with the Arabian Horse Association. In order to find out if this filly is purebred and if she was ever registered, we'll need to send in some hair from her mane to be DNA tested. If she was registered as a foal, they will have a set of her DNA and the results will tell us who she is and how she is bred. That information gives you a good idea of what kind of horse she is likely to be when she is fully grown."

"Won't it hurt if we pull hair from her mane?" interrupted Jillian, with a concerned look.

"No, it doesn't hurt," answered Jennifer, "We pull a few strands and make sure the follicle of the hair is included and then send them to the lab for DNA testing. If Hank registered the mare you should be able to order a copy of her pedigree…"

"This is one of the biggest problems we find with rescue Arabians and other purebreds these days—their prior owners or breeders don't or won't give up their registration papers. This limits the horse's value and usability. It is really frustrating how much harder it is to adopt out an unregistered purebred horse." Jennifer was talking faster, and Jillian admired this passionate woman with a knack not only for helping horses but also for sharing her knowledge.

"It's likely that this one is a purebred though," Jennifer continued, looking at the mare.

"How can you tell?" asked Jillian.

"Well, there are several breed characteristics that are strong in purebred Arabians. First of all, see this space on her forehead between her eyes where it kind of bulges out? And when you turn her head in profile," she turned the mare's head to demonstrate, "you can see her dish-shaped face. That bulge is called the 'jibbah.' It's said that the jibbah allows extra room in her skull for a larger brain.

"Arabians also have wide nostrils that flare and draw in great breaths of desert air. This makes them really successful endurance horses. She has a short, strong back and a long, arched neck. You see where the neck meets her jowl here?" Jennifer pointed to the spot where the mare's cheek met her neck. "This is called her throatlatch. She is very thin, but she has a clean, lovely throatlatch. It is narrow, and when she gets excited or interested, she will be able to snake her neck out."

"I know just what you mean," exclaimed Jillian. She had noticed it yesterday when she brought water to the filly when she was still stuck in the pen. Her neck had indeed stretched out. It seemed to get exceptionally long.

"Another Arabian characteristic is these cute, little pointed ears. They curve toward each other at the top. Ears like that are called 'tippy,' and those tips can be really curly when they are babies. She has beautiful ears," Jennifer continued, as she stroked the mare's neck and rubbed her ears. "She also has lovely Arabian eyes. They are widely spaced apart, and the eyeball and eye bone are protruding or sticking out. Can you see what I mean?"

Jillian was studying the mare's face and could certainly see how big her eyes were and how dainty her ears seemed. From her nostrils to her cheekbones, her muzzle started out small and spread out almost like a V. Her eyes were at the widest part, and then her head began to narrow at the top where her pointy ears were pricked forward as if she knew they were talking about her.

"How do you know so much about Arabian horses?" asked Jillian. "I mean, do you have to study all the breeds and know this much about them all?"

Jennifer smiled. "When I was a girl, I had a half-Arabian and half-Welsh pony. I named her Lulu Belle." She closed her eyes as a warm look flushed her face. When she looked at Jillian again, she was beaming at the memory. "That little pony took me everywhere. We went on trail rides in the desert, swimming at Lake Pleasant, and to all kinds of fun horse shows and barrel racing events. We weren't the fastest, but she was a great pony. We used to show in costume classes; she would wear anything I put on her. She was something special. I wish I had her for my kids," she added wistfully.

"I'm sorry," answered Jillian, assuming that the pony had recently died.

"Oh, gosh, don't be sorry! She passed on years ago. I got her when I was twelve, and she was eleven. Lulu Belle lived to be twenty-eight years old. She had a great life, and I loved her so much. I miss her, but I get to love on horses every day, and I get to help them find great homes now too," Jennifer replied, turning to the filly.

"Since you asked about her age, we would normally have to look at her teeth, but I can tell just by looking that she is close to her third year. See the bumps on the bottom of her jaw? Those are her adult teeth. They form in the bone under her jaw and then make their way up and push out the baby teeth. When her adult teeth are all in, the bumps will be gone."

Jillian marveled at the way horse's teeth grew, and she was glad humans didn't develop adult teeth the same way. She'd look pretty awful with lumps on her bottom jaw.

Jennifer pulled back the mare's lips to look at her front teeth. "She has nice straight teeth and a clean bite. Notice how her teeth meet together in the front? That's good. And yup, she looks about three. She is a bit small for a three-year-old, but when she begins to get good nutrition, she will fatten up and fill out." Suddenly, Jennifer stuck her fingers in the horse's mouth, right along the side.

"What are you doing? Be careful!" Jillian blurted.

"Not to worry," replied Jennifer. "Here, take a look. She has teeth in the front for ripping grass and molars in the back to chew and grind, but there is a little gap here. That is where the bit will go when she wears a bridle," she said, removing her fingers. "We'll have the vet take a look at her teeth when he comes by. She likely has some spots that need filing."

"What do you mean, filing? Like a nail file?" asked Jillian, almost giggling at the idea of how useless a nail file would be in the huge jaw of a horse.

"It's more like a rasp. A metal tool with bumps on it. The tools they have now are electric and the raspy part vibrates and helps to grind down the pointy parts of the teeth," explained Jennifer.

"Wild horses eat grass and plants all day. In the course of grazing, they're constantly grinding their food, and thus, their teeth. In nature, horses don't need dental work, but when they live in captivity, they only eat two times a day. That means their teeth don't get ground down like they do in the wild. A horse with dental 'points' as they are called, can have a hard time eating properly, and it is one of the reasons horses lose weight. Also, when horses are ridden, we extract their wolf teeth, although not every horse develops them. The wolf teeth are like our incisors and they grow in that empty spot behind their front teeth. They don't grow as large as the other teeth. It can be very painful for a horse to carry a bit if they have wolf teeth or other dental problems. And only about 70% of horses even get wolf teeth. Lucky for her, I don't feel one, but we'll have her examined anyway.

"Dr. Longton is our vet. He will be coming out to give her some shots and examine her in a week or so. We want to give her time to get physically on course before we introduce worming and shots."

Jillian was glad Jennifer was organizing the horse's care. She realized how little she knew about horses in comparison.

Bill watched Jillian asking questions. He saw an intelligence that was tempered by empathy; she truly cared about how the horse felt and wanted to learn all she could. She reminded him of Clara. She had the biggest heart of any woman he knew. Clara was forever thinking about other people. Even when she was in the hospital after her spinal surgery, she didn't want to tax the busy nurses. She made close relationships so quickly—everyone loved her. She was more apt to notice the frailties and struggles people hide, and she drew those people out with her warmth and humor.

From what he'd observed, Jillian shared Clara's ability to hone in on how people and animals were feeling.

Bill and Clara had met thirty years earlier when they were in their twenties. He had been driving for a trucking company and she worked as the dispatcher. She had such a sunny character and open sense of humor that every guy in the company had a secret crush on her. She was beautiful in a different way than most women. Clara had suffered from polio as a child. As a result, her legs were weak. She'd worked hard in therapy and was able to get around with braces for most of her life. It wasn't until three years ago that she lost the use of her legs entirely. That had been the hardest: seeing his wife, who loved nothing more than to help others, feeling helpless and unable to take care of herself.

If it hadn't been for Clara though, he wouldn't have built the corral and stalls. She had loved horses, and as her legs became less and less useful, she began to find freedom when she was riding. She convinced him to help her find two well-broke horses they could ride. He'd done just that and brought home two quarter horse geldings that had been ranch horses. They were calm and easy going, especially with Clara. Bill was sure they knew how fragile she had become and they carried her with great caution.

Bill also found solace in the peace he felt on the trail with Clara as she happily chattered away next to him. Their time on horseback was precious and far too short. He couldn't keep the horses after she passed. Every time he looked out the window at them, he was flooded with loss and overwhelmed by sadness. He realized that when he looked at the corral now, he didn't see a sad memory of his Clara, but a new memory being created by Jillian and the little Arabian mare.

Horse Thoughts

There is food and shelter here. Safety. Only daytime lonely. The Hair-Faced two-legger is kind, inside. Eater outside. Scary-safe. He brings small green often. Taste makes stronger. I must live. My new herd. They need me.

A fresh two-legger comes. Herd-scented. Many herds. I see your heart, two-legger. Big heart. Many kindness. Smells of Boss. Moves like Boss. She is head mare. Teacher. The Small One listens, finds respect.

This Boss two-legger shines green-happy. Blue-love. Strong-grey. I see the Small One. She leaks sparks of green sounds. Happiness. Her light inside shines. I think… she loves me! She wants me! Oh, my Small One needs me! I feel lines that draw us together: the herd-bond.

CHAPTER 7 - Rescue 101

Jillian was fascinated with all she was learning about horses. "What is the best time to feed her, and how many times per day, and what is the best food? I wish there was pasture here for her to eat."

"More good questions," replied Jennifer with a smile. "It helps first to understand what happens when a horse starves. Like people, they utilize carbohydrates and fats to create energy. In a healthy situation, those carbs and fats are burned, but more are consumed each day to make up for it. When a horse is starved and after its body uses all of the normal energy sources to function, the horse's body begins to consume protein. The horse's muscles and internal organs are made of protein. The longer they are undernourished, or starved, the more protein—and therefore, muscle and internal organs—is used for fuel, until there is nothing left, and the organs shut down and the horse dies. It is a terrible thing to witness."

Jillian's eyes were glistening as she listened to the rescue director explain what had been happening to the sweet horse in front of her. Her imagination got the better of her, and she could almost feel how hungry the poor girl had been. "How bad is she?" she asked in a quiet voice. "Is she going to die?"

"No, Jillian. She's not going to die. You found her in time. You saved her." Jennifer put a reassuring hand on Jillian's shoulder. "I think this girl is going to be fine. We just need to take it slowly. She is lucky to have the two of you to help her," she said.

"We use something called the 'Henneke body scoring system' to rate the condition of horses. It's a scale from one to nine. A normal, healthy horse is between a five and six. This girl would be rated with a body score of around two. She is pretty thin, but she can be brought back to perfect health, with time and dedication.

"As far as how often to feed her, give her frequent but smaller meals at first. It's better for her system. If you put a bunch of rich food in front of a starving horse, they will eat until they get sick. Did you know that horses can't throw up?"

"What do you mean?" asked Jillian.

"Food can only go in one direction in a horse's digestive system. Horses are grazing animals. In the wild, they eat food all day. They eat and walk and eat and walk and always have something in their stomachs. Horses have two valves in their stomach: one at the beginning and one at the end. Each valve only opens in one direction. They literally are not capable of bringing up food because the valve closes and stops anything from coming back up. Horses have acidic stomach juices to digest their food, and the valve protects their esophagus. This valve becomes a problem when the horse has gas or issues with their stomach or intestines. When their digestion is affected it causes discomfort and can be very dangerous. Since there is only one way for food to go, if a horse has a blockage in their system, they can die. The term, 'colic,' is a generic word used to describe a horse with belly pain."

Jillian had been stroking the filly's forehead but the last three words caused her to freeze. She looked up at Jennifer. "What do you mean they can die? Can't a vet do anything?" Jillian furrowed her brows. "We need to be extra careful with her," she added, stroking the mare once again.

"Depending on the reason for the problem, yes, a vet can help most of the time. If it is gas colic or a light blockage, the veterinarian will put a long plastic tube through the horse's nostril and will guide it down into their stomach. Then they pump oil and/or water into its stomach to help pass the blockage. It is important to keep a colicking horse on its feet. Because they have a stomach ache, many want to lay down, but if they roll around to try to get comfortable, they can sometimes flip their intestines around so they are twisted. This can be very serious and is likely to require surgery."

"Whoa! I didn't know that about horses at all. I thought they were pretty tough. Sticking a tube up her nose sounds gross." She thought a moment, and then asked, "Do horses really let you do that?"

"Not usually," replied Jennifer. "The vet normally sedates the horse before tubing. As soon as we see any sign of colic, we give the horse some Banamine. It is a medicine that helps them to relax. Sometimes just giving the horse Banamine and keeping it walking does the trick—if it's just a gas colic."

"Do they get sick or get colic often? What causes it, and how do we make sure the filly doesn't get it?"

"Excellent questions," Jennifer responded with a grin "There are lots of reasons colic can start, but making sure your horses always drinks plenty of water is an important way to help prevent it, especially here in Arizona where it gets really hot. We also use added electrolytes to help replace those that are lost when horses sweat. You can add it to their water or we'll add some to their grain. The saltiness makes them thirsty so then they drink more. Keeping a horse hydrated helps them keep food going through their system.

"Also, remember that I said that horses were designed to graze all day? When we keep them in captivity, most horses kept in barns are fed twice a day: morning and night. Unless they are turned out into a pasture during the day, there is not much in their gut by mid-afternoon. They rely on us to feed them regularly. That is one of the reasons it is important to feed your horses at around the same time each day—so their bodies get used to the schedule of feeding and can regulate their systems to the schedule. If you feed a horse at 6 a.m. today and 6 p.m. tonight, and then at 11 a.m. tomorrow and 2 p.m., and then the next day at 8 a.m. and 4 p.m., your horses won't know when their next meal is coming and they are more likely to colic."

Jillian was amazed at how complex a horse's digestive system was. She would remember this lesson for a long time. She looked at the sand corral, the stall, and the dry desert all around them. "There isn't any pasture here for her at all, so what is the best way to feed the filly, and what kind of food should she eat so she won't get sick?" she asked.

"Well, we begin our re-feeding program by offering about one pound of alfalfa hay— 1/6 of a flake—every few hours for the first three days. Then we make the meals a little bigger and reduce the number of them for the next two weeks until they are eating three times each day.

"We don't feed them anything but alfalfa hay at first. Most horses that are severely undernourished cannot handle too many carbohydrates very quickly, and alfalfa hay has high protein and low carbs. After they're stable, then we'll add additional supplements and begin worming and dental work and stuff like that," finished Jennifer.

"What about her feet?" Jillian asked. "Her hooves seem to be broken and chipped. Do we have to wait for a few weeks to trim them?"

"Not in her case, no. She is stable enough for us to take care of them this week or next. I will have the farrier contact Bill to set the appointment." Jennifer turned to Bill with questioning eyes.

Bill nodded at Jennifer. "Course. Ya got my phone number, so jus' have him call." He pointed to the shed next to the corral where they stood and Jillian could see that it held several bales of hay. "I think it is time to feed 'er," he said. "Why don'tcha get 'er some hay an' feed 'er a little. Then we can give this girl a bath. An' a name. You can't keep calling 'er 'filly' all the time."

Jillian answered. "I've been thinking of names. But if she is an Arabian and is registered and already has a name, shouldn't we wait to see what it is first?"

"I don't think that matters much. Whatcha think, Jennifer?" asked Bill, turning to the rescue director.

"No, I don't think it matters at all. Lots of registered horses are called by different names. It's called their 'barn name' and is like a nickname," Jennifer replied.

"Well, I am going to look on Google to see if I can find an Arabian horse name that I like," decided Jillian, as she went to the shed and brought back some hay.

The filly began nodding her head again as if to say, "Hurry up with my snack!" and Jillian felt herself relax. First, it had been new friends in school, and now she had permission to take care of this little horse. It was the best Jillian had felt in months.

CHAPTER 8 - Mean Girls, Nice Boys

Jillian was up before the alarm again on Tuesday. She showered, dressed, and grabbed her books. She had studied for the math test on Friday, but she was certain that she'd fail. Math was her worst subject, and she planned to ask Aubrey to give her a hand during study period.

Eating her breakfast quickly, she told her grandma she was meeting friends at the bus stop. It wasn't exactly true. The friends she was going to visit were living next door. She didn't like lying to her grandmother. She was afraid if she kept going to "help Bill with his garden," her grandma might get curious. She knew lying was wrong. It made her stomach queasy. But the sweet, abandoned mare next door needed her. All she was doing right now was helping to care for the mare—at this point anyway. There had to be a way to introduce the horse so that her grandma would help her find a way to keep her.

Bill was waiting for her with a brush in hand. "Ready ta give 'er a quick brush 'fore ya hop on the bus?"

"Yup, I sure am." Jillian was eager to spend time next to the mare. Jennifer had helped Bill give her a bath yesterday, and she looked like a different horse. Instead of a dull, reddish brown, her coat was colored like a copper penny. While it wasn't quite glossy, it was clean. Her mane wasn't mud-brown after all. When the dirt was scrubbed away, her mane and forelock were blonde. Jillian thought it was the most beautiful combination of colors she'd ever seen.

The mare nickered at her to get started. Jillian opened the gate, got in the stall, and started brushing. It didn't take long to brush her, so Jillian spent the last few minutes before she had to catch the bus braiding and unbraiding a section of the blonde mane.

"You'd better hit the bus now, kiddo," interrupted Bill, smiling at the girl and the young mare.

"Okay. Thanks, Bill! I'll be back this afternoon" Jillian rinsed her hands in the hose, grabbed her backpack, and headed to the bus stop.

It was only her second bus ride to school, but it was way better than yesterday. Aubrey waved to her as she got on, so instead of sitting right behind the driver, she joined her new friend near the back passing only six or seven kids in the mostly empty rows of seats.

"How are you doing?" asked Aubrey. "Are you ready for school? I mean the exams we have this week. I have two today and one tomorrow and one on Thursday. What about you?" Aubrey almost sounded excited to be taking exams.

"Me? I don't know how I'm going to do. I was going to see if you could give me a hand with math during study period. I totally don't get it, and math has always been my absolute worst class. Can you help me?" Jillian looked at her questioningly.

"Sure!" she said. "Oh, wait. Darn. I can't. I'm supposed to help in the science study hall today and tomorrow. I'm sorry. What is it that you don't understand? Maybe I can help you on the way to and from school?"

"Oh, um, well, the problem is that I just really don't get fractions and how to divide them. I always get it mixed up. Finding reciprocals for the right fraction and I don't know. I just get them turned around."

"Well, I have an easy way to remember how to divide fractions," a boy's voice interrupted.

The boy sitting in front of them had turned. The first thing she noticed was his chocolate brown, curly hair. She had seen him briefly when she walked back to sit next to Aubrey, but he'd been reading, and his hair covered his face. She was surprised to find intelligent green eyes appraising her. When he smiled, he had thin dimples that made her oddly flustered.

"You must be the new girl. Hi, I'm Trace," he started. "I couldn't help but hear that you need help with fractions. I found a neat trick that I can show you and it isn't too hard to remember. That is, I mean, if you want to." He ended a little less sure of himself as he saw Jillian's hesitant expression.

Aubrey jumped in. " Hey, Trace, that's actually a good idea." Turning to Jillian, she continued, "Trace is in accelerated math with me. He would be a good tutor. And, unlike most of the boys in class, he isn't stupid." She threw a grin in his direction.

Finally, Jillian spoke, "Hi. Um, I guess. Sure. If you can help me during study hall, that would be great. Oh, and I'm Jillian." She held out her hand awkwardly.

Trace reached out and took her hand. His felt cool, strong, and just a bit rough. Their shake was brief and seemed kind of grown-up.

"Well, now that's settled," concluded Aubrey. "Trace lives out past me. If you take the last left there and go down the drive, you can see the family's ranch off New River Road. They board horses and take tourists out on rides up in the hills. Don't you, Trace?"

"Yeah, all winter long. It isn't very busy right now, and soon, when summer hits, we won't have any business at all. At least now I get to ride along instead of just mucking stalls," he added, pushing bangs out of his eyes.

Jillian hadn't had many friends her age that were boys. Andy—Janet's little brother—was tolerable, as were a few other brothers of her childhood friends. She felt a little out of her comfort zone. She'd never studied with a boy, but she really needed help, and if Aubrey said he was cool, she would swallow her discomfort and be grateful.

On the way to school, Aubrey and Trace talked about riding in the desert. Trace told a funny story about a tourist who claimed to be a great equestrian, but he fell off his horse three time on the trail. Trace laughed, "We almost tied him to the saddle so we could make it back to the ranch."

When they arrived at school, Trace waved goodbye as Jillian and Aubrey got off the bus.

"Was that Trace Carter you were talking to?" asked Lila, eyebrows raised. They'd just left Aubrey and were walking together to first period.

"Yup. He's going to tutor me in math during study hall."

"Really. Well, just know that Whitney has a thing for Trace." Lila was a wealth of knowledge about all the kids in the seventh grade. She had lived in town for years, and her outgoing personality introduced her to most of the kids in school.

"I'm not interested in him like that," insisted Jillian. "It is just a study hall tutor session. He's going to help me understand fractions and then say 'see ya,' and maybe I won't fail the test on Friday." She was almost positive that's all it was. She had no time for boys, especially now with a horse to take care of and two new friends.

"Yeah, okay, if you say so," replied Lila with a snort. "He is pretty nice from what I know. His family has a ranch, and they board horses and stuff. He keeps to himself mostly. He's kind of quiet, and I know he's smart. Not as smart as Aubrey, but pretty smart. His family has lived at the ranch as long as I've been around. I guess you could pick a worse guy to like."

"I told you. I don't 'like' him. I just need math help," Jillian repeated a little sharply, getting tired of arguing.

First period went by quickly. Jillian began to feel nervous walking to study hall. She wasn't really used to working with boys, except in class when the teacher forced them. She was beginning to think that maybe this tutoring thing wasn't a good idea. Lila glanced at her as they walked down the stairs.

"You're nervous, aren't you? I can tell. Not anything but a tutor sesh, huh? Keep it together, okay? He is just a boy. A cute boy," she couldn't help but tease.

"Of course, I have it together," Jillian said, sounding more sure than she felt. "I've just never had a boy tutor before. That's all."

The study hall was in a large classroom on the first floor. There were eight round wooden-topped tables, each with six hard plastic chairs. Several of the tables were occupied, one of them by Trace. When he saw Jillian enter, he smiled, running his fingers through his bangs.

"Oh, boy. Good luck, kid." Lila patted Jillian on the arm and turned to sit at an empty table.

"Hi, Jillian," Trace said. "Have a seat and we can get started." He waited until she sat in a chair to his right. "I used to have trouble with fractions in the beginning, but multiplication and division of fractions are actually easier than adding and subtracting. Here, let me show you." Trace began writing fractions in his spiral notebook and turned the paper so she could see it. He scooted his chair a little closer and continued on with the lesson.

At first, Jillian had a hard time concentrating, but Trace was acting just like a tutor or friend, and she soon relaxed and became interested in the lesson. She never noticed Whitney and her friends glaring at them from across the room. Had she glanced up, she would have been shocked at the look of anger on Whitney's face.

Lila, however, didn't miss anything. She saw Whitney glower at Jillian and knew she had correctly predicted Whitney's reaction to the math lesson. She kept an eye on the trio that seemed to get more upset by the minute. When Jillian laughed at a joke that Trace had made, she saw Whitney's eyes narrow but was surprised when the stuck-up girl stood and walked over to confront the pair.

"What's the matter, new girl, are you flunking math already?" Whitney spit out, a smug look on her face.

Surprised by the interruption, Jillian stammered, but before she could reply, Trace stood up and faced Whitney. He was at least four inches taller than she was, and his stare was hard and direct. "What's going on here is none of your business, Whitney. Why don't you go back to your friends and leave us alone."

Whitney blanched but wasn't ready to back down. "I came to tell you that my riding club—the Anthem Riding Academy—will be attending the Freedom Ride next weekend when school is out. So we will be seeing you at your ranch. Won't that be fun? You can be our guide." She smiled at Trace and leaned toward him. "I'm sure you'll have more fun guiding us around the desert than tutoring dumb girls in school," she said, loud enough for the whole room to hear. Then Whitney gave Jillian a cool smile, flipped her blonde hair off her shoulder, spun around, and stalked off.

Jillian was shocked. Lila had warned her, but she didn't understand why someone she'd just met could hate her so much. Her face flushed red and then paled to white, her freckles standing out starkly on her blanched skin.

Trace sat down next to her. "I'm so sorry, Jillian. She's a total idiot. What a nasty thing to say." He looked at her, his green eyes blazing. "She's just a bully. Ignore her. School will be done for the year soon enough," he said.

"You know how to wake up a room, girl!" Lila pointed out at the end of class. She sat down in the chair next to Jillian. "Didn't I tell you? That chick is nuts. I think you might have made an enemy."

"I don't want to be anyone's enemy, Lila. I'm not used to being bullied. I was... I mean, I had more friends at home in Washington," Jillian faltered, feeling a wave of unwanted loneliness despite the concerns of the two other kids at the table.

Sensing her discomfort, Lila stood up. "We'd better get going. Study Hall is over, and I need to dump my books at my locker. C'mon, Jillian."

Jillian turned to Trace. "Thanks for the lesson, Trace. It really did help. I don't know how you understand it so well, but now I feel a little better about the test. And sorry for, you know, Whitney."

"It's cool. Let me know if you have any more questions. I'll tutor you anytime. Don't worry about Miss Priss. She's an idiot. I've got gym now, so I'll see you on the bus." Trace smiled at Jillian, winked at Lila, and left.

Unfortunately, Whitney was in most of her classes and Jillian spent the rest of the day trying her best to avoid her. She didn't want to get into any hassles. It was hard enough being the new girl.

It wasn't until the last class of the day that Jillian heard Whitney say, "Hey, Red. You know something? You remind me of Ronald McDonald! You know, the clown, red frizzy hair, dumb expression, works at McDonald's." Whitney laughed as she paused next to Jillian who was seated in social studies. Some of the kids nearby giggled. Some ignored Whitney knowing they could be her next target.

But Aubrey, who'd walked in right behind Whitney, immediately quipped back, "You're the only clown in this room, Blondie. Now go sit down and quit making a fool of yourself." At 5'6", Aubrey was intimidating, and as she moved closer to the indignant bully—hands on hips, eyes blazing—Whitney shrunk back.

"You're a geek yourself," Whitney hissed, looking miffed and unsettled. Taking her seat next to her two friends, she smoothed her blond locks as her friends cooed and clucked over her.

Grateful for the backup, Jillian smiled at Aubrey who returned the smile with a big grin. Thankfully, school was almost over. Only one and a half more weeks.

CHAPTER 9 - Heartstrings

Jillian woke up on Saturday morning well before her alarm was set to ring at 6:30 a.m. She shifted in her bed trying to get comfortable so she could fall back to sleep. She had completed her first week of school and most of her exams. Seattle and Arizona schools were not that different, but she wasn't sure she'd done all that well on her tests. It was a strange feeling because, growing up in Woodinville, she was always at the top of her class. She was one of the lucky kids who didn't have to study too hard to understand the material—in every class but math. But now the math test was over and she actually thought she'd passed. The advice Trace gave her during the week had made a difference.

She'd mostly avoided Whitney and her mean girl crowd with help from Aubrey and Lila. Thank goodness for them! She couldn't have found nicer friends. It would have been so much harder if she hadn't met them. Together only one week, they felt like three peas in a pod; life almost felt normal and Jillian felt herself slowly opening up. Lila was silly and made her laugh. It was easy to find things to laugh about when she was around Lila. Not as much when she was at home, except when she was helping with the mare. Aubrey's serene air and sharp intelligence masked her sometimes goofy wit. With the support of both friends, Jillian's first week in her new school was tolerable.

In addition to the studying for exams, Jillian had been researching names for Arabian horses and was captivated by the translations. She searched through the meanings of the names and found some that were perfect in meaning, but were hard to pronounce or too long. She had narrowed it down to *Jamila*: Beautiful or *Kalila*: Sweetheart.

Jillian had yet to tell her friends about the mare. She'd thought about it several times in the last week and had almost said something twice. But for some reason, she wanted to hold on to the secret just a bit longer. She had decided she would tell them today when she went to Aubrey's house for the first time. They were going riding; well, at least two of them were riding. Aubrey only had two horses, so they decided they would take turns walking and riding. Jillian hadn't been riding since her parents took her to Ocean Shores last summer. They'd taken a trail ride on the beach, and even though the horses had seemed bored with the whole outing, she thought it was fun and was looking forward to riding again. She only hoped she wouldn't do something stupid like fall off or lose control of the horse like her father had that one time.

They were on their annual weeklong July vacation on the coast in Ocean Shores, Washington. It was a cool morning, but the low overcast skies promised to clear, and she was ready to go out on the trail. She had been given a big black and white horse named Gus. He was not the prettiest horse, nor was he the youngest, but she thought he was beautiful, and as they readied for the ride, she sat in the saddle stroking his neck and admiring his half-black, half-white mane.

Her mom got on a pretty brown mare with a black mane and tail. The guide said the horse's color was called "bay." Her dad's mare was red, and she discovered they called the color "chestnut." That didn't make much sense to her. All the chestnuts she'd seen were not red—they were brown. They tasted yummy when they were roasted over the fire, but they weren't red. She meant to ask the guide about the reason for the name but was distracted by the turn of events.

The ride had begun easily enough. They were in a group of seven riders plus the guide. Another family of four joined them, but the kids were in their teens and the whole family seemed to know how to ride. They wound their way single file down the trail from the stable, and through a small stand of trees toward the beach. They rode over dunes of sand and spiky grass until they topped a rise and saw the Pacific Ocean spread out before them. It was like a beautiful dark blue blanket with white fringe that kept moving on and off the sand. The family that rode ahead of them spurred their horses into a trot toward the ocean's edge.

"Whoa!" cried the trail guide. "Whoa, please no trotting or cantering yet!" But his voice was carried off by the strong breeze that blew in the wrong direction, and the four horses ahead sped up to a gallop. The guide tried to move from behind her mom to the front of their much shortened line, but Dad's horse had a different idea. She took the bit in her mouth and bolted off after the other horses. The look of surprise on Dad's face was almost hilarious except for the fact that he was bouncing on the saddle and holding onto the horn for dear life.

The guide yelled, "Pull up on the reins! Pull hard!" and Jillian could see her dad trying to follow his instructions. It took him a while, but he was finally able to gain control by pulling harder on his right rein and causing the horse to make a big circle. He pulled her up in front of the guide with a look of combined terror, embarrassment, and a tinge of pride.

"Well done," exclaimed the guide. "Well done. Now, let's just walk along the shoreline for a while, okay? We'll take it easy."

"Yeah, take it easy. Ha!" her dad countered, shaking his head.

"Nice ride, Dad!" she'd said to him, and her mom burst out laughing and spent the rest of the ride calling him "Lone

Ranger" and saying "High-ho Silver!" Jillian didn't get the joke, but her mom had a great time teasing her dad.

The memory was so clear it felt like it was only yesterday. But her life was totally changed now. The image of that day on the beach disappeared, and the ceiling in her real-life bedroom came sharply into focus. Jillian got out of bed deciding that staying still wasn't a good idea. She had too many memories when she lay there alone in her room. It was time to get ready for her ride.

"Do you want two pancakes or three?" Grandma Allison asked Jillian when she got to the kitchen. Her grandma was an early riser and beat Jillian to the kitchen every day. She had been conditioned by all her years working at the post office when she had gone to work at 5 a.m.

"Three sounds great, Grandma. Thanks," replied Jillian. "You remember that I'm going to Aubrey's house today to go horseback riding and swimming in her pool. Aubrey's mom is going to pick me up at nine and drop me off about six tonight."

"I remember," answered Allison with a smile. "I'm so glad you found some nice girls to play with. You have to promise to wear a helmet when you ride. And don't swim after you eat lunch for at least an hour, okay?"

"Okay, Grandma. Don't worry," Jillian replied with a tiny eye roll followed by a grin.

"I have something important to talk to you about, Jillian," said Allison, as she sat across the kitchen table from Jillian, coffee cup in hand. "I got some mail from your parents' estate lawyer, Mr. Steiner. It seems your mom and dad set up a fund for you. They wanted to help pay for your expenses and so the lawyers will be sending us a check for $2,000 each month."

"$2,000 a month? That seems like a lot," Jillian replied.

"Well, they wanted you to get $400 of it to spend yourself, and then I am to use the rest of the money for clothes and food and activities for you. I have to tell you that I was honestly surprised. I feel so disappointed I didn't spend more time with your family when you lived in Washington. I wish, oh, how I wish I could turn back time." Grandma Allison swallowed hard and wiped a tear from her cheek. "They also did something incredible for me. They paid off the mortgage on this house so we never have to worry about not having a home. This will be your home from now until you are ready to go to college. I'm so grateful for their generosity. It just breaks my heart that they're gone."

Jillian couldn't hold back her own tears. She hadn't started out feeling very close to her grandma, but the last weeks had taught her a lot about the woman who raised her mom; she'd gained more respect and affection for her each day. Her grandma was a kind person, and she could see her mom in many of the older woman's expressions and mannerisms.

Jillian stood up, blinking rapidly, and went to Allison, and crawled into her lap. She wrapped her arms around Allison's neck and began to weep. They clung together, the red-haired orphan girl and the grey-haired woman, sharing their grief and mutual loss. It felt so good to be held that Jillian realized she'd almost forgotten how comforting it was to feel someone's arms around her. She let down her guard and allowed her tears to flow.

Aaron was about to enter the room when he saw the two embracing. He felt a quick flush of anger. That girl was buying her way into his mother's affection! She had only been here a month and already she was being treated like the favorite. He had helped his mother all these years, and she was never as grateful to him. He almost let his anger get the best of him, but he knew he'd have to play nice if he wanted to share in Jillian's inheritance. He longed to quit working and spend his time with his pals at the bar. It burned him to do it, but he pulled a fake smile together and walked into the kitchen.

"Mornin'. What's goin' on? You girls havin' a cry-fest or something?" he couldn't help saying. Jillian stood up and went back to her seat. She started eating her cold pancakes ignoring Aaron's snide comment.

"Aaron, don't be so mean. We were talking about your sister," Allison said, standing up and heading to the sink to rinse her cup.

"Well, she ain't here anymore, is she? And she ain't coming back. No point in crying. I'm just sayin'."

"Aaron! Don't speak like that about your sister. What an awful thing to say. Show some respect" Allison saw Jillian's face go red. Aaron noticed too, and his thin mouth turned slightly up at the ends.

"I have to go, Grandma. I promised Bill I would help him plant some flowers." Jillian hated the way Aaron talked to Grandma Allison. If she'd talked to her mom like that she would have been in big trouble. It was weird that her grandma, who was tough in some ways, would let her son speak to her like that.

Jillian had to get out of there. "I'll be back before nine to meet Mrs. McKinstry." Jillian fled the kitchen and the thick feeling of resentment that emanated from her uncle. She didn't know why he hated her so much. He didn't even know her.

Aaron walked to the coffee pot and poured himself a cup. He said nothing, but he wondered why Bill would need help gardening at 7:30 on a Saturday morning. Ignoring his mother's angry glare, he took his cup with him and wandered outside. Standing on the patio and blowing on his steaming mug, he looked down the road and up the other side. There she was. He caught a glimpse of her blue t-shirt as she walked down the neighbor's driveway. Curious about why his niece would be visiting his neighbor this early, Aaron followed.

Jillian skipped down Bill's driveway to the corral and the young mare nickered when she saw Jillian. Jillian attempted a nicker back.

"Not too bad, kid," said Bill, as he stepped out of the shed. He had been organizing the latest load of hay and supplies Jennifer had dropped off yesterday. "Ya ready to give 'er a groomin'?" he asked, knowing the answer already.

"Yup, I sure am!" Jillian replied. "And, guess what? I decided on a name. I wanted something that described her but was in Arabic because she is an Arabian. Google Translate helped me, and I picked 'Jamila' which means 'beautiful.'"

"Jamila," repeated Bill. "I like the way that rolls off the tongue. I think it's a great name for 'er, an' she sure is a beauty."

Jamila began to toss her head as if in agreement, and Jillian gave her a scratch on her neck.

"Yes, you are beautiful, my girl," she murmured to the mare. Jillian was amazed at the change in the horse in just under a week. Her chestnut coat was no longer dull, and while you could still see her ribs and hip bones, her head didn't seem as oversized as it had, and she somehow looked taller. "And now I have to clean your stall, my friend, so back away from the door please, and I'll be right in."

Bill handed her a blue manure bucket and red tined pitchfork, then slid back the bolt to the corral gate. Jamila had a twelve-by-twelve-foot covered stall near the gate, and the corral was about twenty feet wide and thirty feet long. The sand in the corral and stall made it easy to pick up the poop, and Jillian found herself humming tunelessly under her breath. She never thought that cleaning up after an animal could be so rewarding. She caught herself thinking of her mom and the way she used to hum when she cooked. Maybe humming while you work was a family tradition. The thought made her smile.

When she'd finished scooping the stall, she checked the big galvanized tank that held water. It was three-quarters of the way full. "Should I fill the water, Bill?" she called out, catching Bill as he was walking toward the house.

Bill turned to answer and saw something out of the corner of his eye that made him look up his driveway. He could have sworn he saw someone there, but he scanned the driveway and road and didn't see anything. Musta' been a shadow, he thought.

"Yeah, why not fill it up, please," Bill responded. "Just in case she plays in it. She has been havin' a blast splashin' in 'er water, but she gits it all sandy an' muddy. She likes the tub half-full when she turns it inta a pony pool. Maybe, if we keep it full, she won't wanna play in it so much."

"I groomed her a little this morning, but if ya wanna brush out 'er mane an' forelock, that'd be great. You're goin' off on a play date, right?" he asked.

"It isn't called a 'play date' anymore, Bill," Jillian said with a roll of her eyes. "We're twelve you know. Play dates are for when you are under five. Seriously. We're going to go riding. My friends Aubrey and Lila and me. I can't wait!"

Her enthusiasm made Bill smile, again finding himself grateful for the young spark that had entered his life. "Ya better finish up quick an' get to ridin'. That sounds like way more fun than scoopin' stalls." He smiled at her again, and with a fruitless glance up the driveway, he turned to head inside.

"Before you go, Bill, I wanted to ask you something." Jillian stopped him with her question.

Bill turned. "What's that, Jillian?"

"Well, I wonder if you know how much it costs to adopt a horse? See, I found out this morning that my parents left me some money. I get $400 each month just to spend on what I want."

Bill's eyes widened at this news. "That sure is some good news fer ya, young lady! I don't know what Healin' Horses charges fer adoption, but let's not get too far ahead of ourselves. We need ta get this mare nice an' healthy first. But I think that Jennifer likes ya, an' from what I know the adoption fees aren't too steep," he added with a smile.

"And can I, I mean is it okay if she stays here?" asked Jillian. "I can pay you for her food and give you some money to help me take care of her. I mean, if you don't mind me coming over too much…" Jillian let the sentence drop, looking down feeling embarrassed and realizing she had taken it for granted that Bill would help.

"Course she kin stay here, but I know ya haven't told yer grandma yet, an' she'll need to okay it before I kin really say yes," Bill reminded her.

"I know." Jillian looked serious. "I need to tell her. But what if she says no? And what if Uncle Aaron hates Jamila or does something to her? I'd never forgive myself."

"Now don't go makin' problems where there aren't any," said Bill. "Jus' be honest with yer grandma. She's a reasonable person, an' I'm sure she'll see how much ya love Jamila. I think she'll come around. And as far as Aaron," he said, his face darkening, "ya jus' leave 'em to me. He won't hurt this horse long as I'm around."

Jillian felt relieved. She knew she had to tell Grandma Allison. She would tell her right after the ride.

Neither Jillian nor Bill noticed the figure hiding behind the big Saguaro and hibiscus bush scowling at what he had heard.

Gardening! Ha. What a little sneak she is. As they chattered on, Aaron belly crawled along the low stucco wall until he was out of sight of the corral. He got up fuming.

That stupid kid was gonna spend all their money! Horses ain't cheap. And what if it needs to go to the vet? Vets are expensive. She'd spend all their money on that bag of bones. And that idiot neighbor was doing nothin' to stop her. He thinks he can take care of me? Ha! He has no idea what I can do.

Aaron headed home determined to put an end to this ridiculous obsession of Jillian's. Yeah, end it… he would find a way.

Jamila's Thoughts

My Small One! Breath-is-my-breath. Heart-is-my-heart. Her loneliness is no longer. More love. Shared secrets. Soft scented innocence. Her love shines blue-bright! She sees. She knows. She feels.

The herd replaced. Small and big. Safety. Oh, the water! Drink. Play. Cool. Full. Every day green. True as the sun. Gnawing pangs gone. Touching is love. Scratches bond. The Small One goes deep. We connect: not just herd-bond. A love-bond. She named me! Herd-safe name. Heart-safe name. Joy! Play! Touch!

They clean and make fresh. The Small One leaks sounds, low and soft. Her sounds are many. She feels the sounds. Can she see mine? I send warm blue of comfort. Love.

Attention! Danger! Scent of Eater-Man anger. There. The sharp yellow shadow. Warning! Listen. It withdraws. Rage lingers close. Be wary Small One. Some two-leggers have two faces.

CHAPTER 10 – A Poopy Tale

Aubrey and her mom had just pulled into the driveway when Jillian got home. She waved, then ran inside to get her backpack. Grandma Allison was in the kitchen, and she followed Jillian to their truck introducing herself to Mrs. McKinstry and getting her phone number. "Have fun and be safe!" she called after them and turned back to the house.

Jillian was surprised how close to Aubrey she lived. It was less than a five-minute drive from Grandma's to the McKinstry house. She could walk there in half an hour or less.

Built of stucco, like many Arizona homes, theirs was large and beautifully maintained. Aubrey's two Labradors met them with brown eyes shining and black tails wagging at the arched door of the covered portico. Aubrey's little sister Zoe shyly said hello as the older girls passed through the living room. High ceilings and tall windows revealed a backyard that blazed with color. Roses, sunflowers, blooming cactus and all manner of flowers were planted around the pool. It was delightful and unexpected to see all that color in the desert, and it reminded her of Bill's yard.

With a Buddha statue on one side and a slide on the other, it was clear both children and adults enjoyed the pool. A Ping-Pong table and built-in barbeque completed the awesome entertainment space. Jillian felt an unwanted tinge of jealousy. Her old life in Washington had been much like this, with two loving parents who worked hard to provide for their kids and create an atmosphere of love and support. She missed the feeling of home.

Mrs. McKinstry hung up her cell phone as she closed the front door behind her. "That was Lila's mom. Sounds like

Lila has a fever and isn't feeling well. She won't be able to come today, so it's just the two of you."

"Thanks, Mom. That's too bad. I hope she feels better." Turning to her friend, Aubrey suggested, "Let's go to my room and we can plan our day, okay?"

"Sure! That sounds great." Jillian followed Aubrey across the tiled floor and through the sliding door. She led Jillian to the right of the wide stone patio, its padded wicker furniture upholstered in Hawaiian print pillows that looked like the kind you could sink into and take a nap.

Aubrey's room reminded Jillian a bit of her own room in Woodinville. She'd had her own bath, just like Aubrey, and her room was down a hallway from the main bustle of the house.

A big painting of a young, dark grey Arabian horse on a pinkish background dominated the wall over Aubrey's bed, and she had several photos and decorations that were of Parisian design. The overall effect was one of sophistication and intelligence, much like the inhabitant of the room. Jillian liked it right away.

"This is a cool room," she exclaimed, looking around with glee. The windows opened to the backyard, and Jillian glimpsed the paddock in the back. "Which horse is yours?" she asked Aubrey, as they stood together looking out the window.

"The black and white mare is mine. She is half-Saddlebred and half-Arabian. Her name is Grace," Aubrey explained. "Our other horse, Amora, is a purebred Arabian that belongs to my mom. She is lots older—almost fifteen, I think. We'll go out and get ready for the ride soon." They turned and Jillian studied the room some more.

She noticed the bookshelves were crammed with all sorts of books from horse stories to science fiction and lots of young adult novels. She felt that nostalgic twinge again remembering her own book collection. She wondered where it was and if she would ever get them back, or would they be sold or dumped with the rest of her old household furnishings. Aubrey brought her out of her reverie asking, "What kind of books do you like to read?"

Jillian thought for a moment and answered, "Mostly science fantasy like *Harry Potter* and *Lord of the Rings*. I loved the Miss Peregrine books and *The Lion Witch and the Wardrobe*. That kind of stuff. You are lucky to have so many books. I wish I still had mine." Jillian stopped herself turning to sit on the bed. "So tell me what it's like to have a horse? How old is she?"

"Grace is five and she is super sweet, but she can get into trouble. In fact, she kind of gets into a lot of trouble on a regular basis," she chuckled. "She's figured out how to close the stall gates, and she likes to lock Amora in her stall and steal her hay, or do it just to see Amora get mad. It's pretty hilarious but not a great habit. We have to snap-lock all the corral gates so she doesn't escape. Mom calls her 'Houdini Girl.'" Aubrey giggled and it lightened the mood. "Taking care of her isn't really hard, but it is kind of a pain when we want to go anywhere. Or, if I want to do other things, I have to make sure I get Zoe or Mom or Dad to cover my chores. Cleaning poop isn't my favorite thing, but she just keeps pooping!" Jillian was giggling now too.

"Did you know that horses poop between ten and twelve times a day? That means when I clean the stalls and turnout, I have to pick up more than twenty poops!" Aubrey crinkled her nose. "At least it doesn't smell too horrible. Not as bad as dog poop or chicken poop. I have to clean those up too. I guess I live a poopy life," she exclaimed, laughing so contagiously that Jillian couldn't help but to join in imagining Aubrey surrounded with piles of poo.

"Do you know if it costs a lot to take care of your horses?" Jillian was hoping she had enough money to care for Jamila.

"The horses are pretty expensive to keep. Mom and I add up how much we spend on hay and grain, hoof care, dental work and vaccines each year. It's about $250 per horse, per month. That doesn't include any emergency vet visit or training or horse showing. I'm super lucky to be able to keep horses in my backyard. I have some friends I ride with and they pay to have their horses boarded at a stable; it costs them $500 a month without any training. It's expensive!"

Jillian realized she hadn't thought about all the costs associated with caring for a horse. She was suddenly grateful for what Grandma Allison told her this morning. She would be getting $400 per month, so if she spent a little more than half on the horse, she'd still be able to have plenty of money if she needed it. She would save the rest in case of an emergency. She thought about Old Hank and his creepy son. The rescue had picked up eight horses from the property. That meant Hank used to spend more than a fifteen hundred dollars a month to take care of them. His jerk of a son probably just didn't want to spend the money and figured he'd let them die. The thought made Jillian angry. How could someone just stop feeding their horse? It would be like not feeding your dog or kid.

Jillian started talking without thinking. "Last weekend I heard a neighbor had died and left a bunch of Arabian horses. His son didn't feed them or take care of them and I went next door when my uncle told me about it. There was a rescue group picking them up. The poor things didn't have any food or water. It was awful." Jillian shared the drama of watching the confrontation between Hank's son and Jennifer from Healing Horses. Before she knew it, she was talking about Jamila. "I was sitting there on a big rock next to the property and I heard a noise. It kind of spooked me at first, but I had to go see what it was, and you won't believe it but there was a young mare trapped under the collapsed metal roof of the junky old shelter."

"What? You mean there was a horse trapped there?" asked Aubrey, frowning.

"Exactly," replied Jillian. "I didn't know what to do. I was able to get most of the corrugated roofing off of her and found a cracked bucket and gave her some water. Then I went to pick grass and almost got bitten by a rattlesnake."

"What? I hate snakes! What happened? What do you mean, 'almost got bitten?'" Aubrey demanded.

"Well, that's when it got exciting. My other neighbor, Bill, showed up at just the right time and grabbed an old shovel and chopped off its head! It was gross and I was like 'who the heck is this guy and is he going to hurt me too?' Luckily, he's a really nice man and he helped me get the mare up and to his house, and now we're taking care of her." Jillian realized she had just spilled the beans about Jamila. It felt good to tell someone. Aubrey was regarding her with a look of surprise.

"Wait a minute. Are you telling me that you have a horse of your own too? Really? Wow! That's great!"

"Not exactly great, and she's not my own, not right now anyway," replied Jillian with a guilty look. "My grandma doesn't know about the horse yet. I mean when Uncle Aaron told me about the horses up the street, he said they should all be shot. I'm scared he'll try to hurt her. And Grandma doesn't know anything about horses, and she might not want her either. I'm afraid that if I tell, they'll make her go to the rescue.

You and Bill and the lady who runs the rescue are the only ones who know. I've been meaning to tell you," she faltered, looking at the bedspread. "I'm sorry I didn't say anything earlier. I haven't told Lila yet either. I didn't know if I'd be able to keep the horse, and I still don't know."

"Well, aren't you full of surprises! So is the neighbor helping you take care of her? What is her name? And she is an Arabian? Is that why you were asking me questions about taking care of a horse?"

"Yes, I guess it is," admitted Jillian. "I really don't know very much, and I want to take good care of her. Do you think you could give me some pointers?"

" I am sure I can," replied Aubrey excitedly. "We can have 'horse camp,' and I can teach you all about them."

"She is an Arabian, and Jennifer from the rescue told me she's around three years old, even though she is pretty small. Horse camp sounds awesome," Jillian grinned back at her new friend. She was relieved and happy. She had friends, she had Jamila, and her grandma was trying hard to make her happy. She felt a slender spark of hope.

CHAPTER 11 - Hoof Picks, Horns, and Horses

Aubrey promised to keep Jillian's secret about the mare. She also agreed to come to visit and offer what advice she could. She was excited to meet the mysterious horse.

"So you keep calling her 'the mare.' Does that mean that you haven't got a name yet?" asked Aubrey.

"Well, since she is an Arabian, I did a Google Translate on some words in Arabic, and I decided to name her 'Jamila,' which means beautiful."

"I like it. A beautiful name for a beautiful horse. Do you think I can come by next weekend for the first day of horse camp?" questioned Aubrey with a grin.

"Yes! That would be great. I just have to tell Grandma about Jamila first." Jillian was feeling a little guilty. She knew she would have to tell her grandmother. She didn't like keeping the horse a secret, but it wasn't like she was the only one taking care of her. Bill was the one who was really keeping her.

Aubrey jumped up. "We can start a lesson right now," she exclaimed. "Let's go out and see the horses. I'll teach you how to groom them. We can get them brushed up, and I'll show you how to put on the bridle and saddle. Mom said we could go for a short trail ride, but only to the spot where the trail crosses the road. Then we have to come back. It will still be super fun."

Jillian giggled. *This was going to be exciting!*

The horses were waiting for them at the gate when the girls got down to the barn. They were in separate stalls in what Aubrey called a "mare motel." Jillian had heard Bill refer to Jamila's stalls the same way. She thought it was a pretty funny name for a pipe rail enclosure. "Do they have 'mare hotels' too? Or 'gelding motels'?" she asked with a chuckle.

Aubrey groaned. "Oh, geez." She reacted with an exaggerated eye roll, and they laughed together as they approached the horses.

"This girl here is my Grace," introduced Aubrey, as she reached up and straightened the forelock of the striking black and white horse. Grace had beautiful markings. Her mane was half black and half white and she had a crazy-long neck. Her body shone with interlocking dark and light. Grace's dark eyes were lit with intelligence, and she nuzzled Aubrey and reached out to sniff Jillian. "You can pat her. She is really nice. Did you know it is always better to pat a horse you are just meeting on the neck instead of the face? It is safer until you know if the horse nips or not. You can let her smell your hand and then move a little closer to the side to scratch her neck."

Aubrey demonstrated the neck scratch, and Grace lifted her head extending her upper lip and waggling it back and forth. The girls giggled at the sight. "That's her itchy spot. Her silly lip wiggle is a natural reaction. She and Amora will stand side by side facing opposite directions, and they will scratch each other with lip wiggles just like that. Well, until one of them—usually Amora—nips the other hard instead of scratching."

"So, Grace is part Arabian and what else did you tell me?" asked Jillian.

"Yup, her mom's an Arabian and her dad's a Saddlebred. He is black and white like she is. They sometimes call black and white markings 'tobiano' or 'pinto.' Purebred Arabian horses don't come in black and white. They are bay or grey or chestnut. They can have white on their legs and on their face and even splashes of color on their bellies, but they aren't like her."

Moving to the next stall, Aubrey introduced Jillian to Amora, a beautiful bay Arabian mare with a white stripe on her face and three short white socks. Her black mane and forelock were thick and shiny, and she had the same look of intelligence in her eyes that Grace had. "Amora is fifteen, I think. Mom has had her since she was seven. She's a sweetie, but she's a pig! She bosses Grace around all the time."

"But Grace is taller and bigger than she is. How come Amora's the one in charge?" questioned Jillian.

"The size of the boss mare doesn't matter too much. In every horse herd, there is a boss mare. She's the leader, and in the wild, she leads the herd while the stallion follows up the rear. The boss mare is usually older. Horses have a pecking order, kind of like chickens. Some are more dominant than others. One way they show their dominance is by making the other horse move, either by pushing, biting, or sometimes kicking it. The horse that moves is the loser, sort of.

"Because they're herd animals, horses don't like to live alone. They use their pecking order system to keep control of the herd. Even though sometimes it seems mean, it's rare for any of the horses to get seriously hurt. They make a big show, but there's not lots of anger."

Jillian was fascinated to learn about their social structure. She knew horses lived in herds, but she never thought about how they organized themselves. Amora looked at her with curiosity. "She's begging for a treat," said Aubrey, smiling. "She is a big piggy!"

"Well, I think she is a pretty piggy," replied Jillian. With a self-satisfied look, Amora snorted spraying Jillian's shirt with flecks of horse snot. Aubrey burst out laughing and soon the two of them were hooting with glee. Jillian felt great laughing until her sides ached.

"Okay, let's get them groomed and tacked up," directed Aubrey, leading Jillian to the red wooden shed to the right of the stalls. Jillian noticed the large turnout area behind the stalls, and to the left was a corral that had a circle beaten into the sandy dirt.

Aubrey saw Jillian's look of curiosity, and explained, "That circle is where we lunge the horses. Lunging them basically means making them move in a circle around you while they are on a long line. We usually groom the horses, then put on their saddles and bridles, and then lunge them with a halter over the bridle."

"What is the point of lunging them and getting them tired if we are going to ride them anyway?" asked Jillian.

"Lunging does a couple of things. First, it helps warm up the horse. We start out walking, then we trot, then walk, and then canter and then walk again. It helps them to loosen their muscles like we do when we stretch before we run in gym. It also helps the horse get comfortable with the saddle, and you can tell how frisky the horse feels that day. We do that in both directions. It only takes about ten minutes, but it helps, especially with Grace since she is young. And don't worry, it won't tire them out. They have lots of energy." Aubrey smiled.

"So, now let's groom them. You have groomed Jamila, haven't you?" Aubrey asked Jillian.

"Yup, well, mostly. I've brushed her mane and tail and her body, but Bill does her legs and feet," Jillian explained.

"Well, I'll show you how to do that too. Let's get started." Aubrey got out a bucket loaded with brushes and combs, and she showed Jillian how to brush the horse's hair in the direction that it lays. "It isn't super comfortable for the horse if you brush against the direction of the hair. Did you know their skin is sensitive enough to feel a fly land even though it is way thicker than ours in most places?"

Aubrey demonstrated her brushing technique. "Hold the brush in your hand, and at the bottom of each swipe, you kind of flick your wrist to help flip the dirt out of her coat. See?" And she repeated the brush stroke. Jillian found it wasn't hard to master. She brushed Amora on her long neck, remembering Jamila's favorite scratching spots and finding that Amora liked them too.

"Okay, now when you brush her legs, just follow the direction of the hair, and brush her the same way you did her body. See how I'm standing on the side of her to brush her leg? I found out the hard way that it's safer than standing in front. I didn't even think about it 'cause I was bent over looking at her knee when she picked it up and bopped me on the chin. It hurt," she said, widening her eyes indignantly at Jillian's giggle.

Jillian followed the directions and soon both front legs were brushed. As they headed to the back legs, Aubrey explained something she called the "kick zone," which is a swath about three feet or so around the horse's hindquarters.

"Either stay super close to the horse's butt or take a detour around the butt." And she demonstrated with a hop and a skip away from Grace's rear, dancing around to the other side.

"You are a kook, you know?" declared Jillian.

"I know! And I'm proud of my kookiness," answered Aubrey with a cheesy grin. "Okay, let's get these kooky horses' feet cleaned, and we can get ready to ride."

Aubrey took out a hoof pick, a metal L-shaped tool that Jillian recognized. She ran her hand down Grace's front leg giving her a gentle squeeze at the back of her foreleg. Grace picked up her leg, and Aubrey cupped the hoof providing support as she began scraping the hoof pick into the sand and poop that was stuck in there. She worked around the V-shaped center of the hoof. "This is called her 'frog,' you know."

"What do you mean 'frog?' It doesn't look like a frog."

"Well, that's what it's called. They have some sensitivity in their frog, but the outside shell of their hooves is made of the same kind of stuff as our fingernails. The bottom of a horse's foot is tough, but you don't have to go very far up inside the hoof to create problems. That's why we always clean their feet before and after we ride—to make sure no rocks or anything are stuck."

When the hoof was clean, she set down Grace's leg and moved to the rear. "You have to be careful when the horses are young and learning. It takes a little time for them to get used to picking up their hind feet and they sometimes try to pull away. You just have to be patient. Mom says I can't give up if she keeps trying to pull her leg away. I hold on tight, and even if she yanks her leg out of my hands, I start again at her hip and run my hands down her leg slowly until I can pick it up again. Grace is smart. She doesn't fight me anymore, but she did for a while. Here, you do Amora's hind feet, and I'll help."

Jillian found it wasn't as hard or intimidating holding a horse's big hoof and leg as she'd imagined. It was awkward and a little heavy, but Amora was experienced and didn't resist. Jillian finished both hind feet and looked at her friend. "What's next?" she asked.

"Next we are going to tack them up. Come and help me get the saddles," Aubrey answered. There were two different looking saddles in the shed. One was smaller and smooth with leg flaps and metal stirrups hanging on leather straps. The other was bigger and had lots more leather with a knob in the front.

It was the kind of saddle she had ridden in before, and it looked a lot easier to hold on to than the smaller one.

"You grab the English saddle, and I'll get the western one," instructed Aubrey, reaching for the heavier saddle. "This one is going to go on Amora, and the one you have is going on Grace."

"They're so different. I've ridden in the bigger saddle, but I've never seen this other type," admitted Jillian.

"Well, they're each for different disciplines. I ride in the English saddle when I'm training for the hunter-under-saddle classes. Grace doesn't compete in western classes, but Mom used to a little bit with Amora. There are loads of differences between the two kinds of riding. It would take me a long time to explain everything, but I saw you eyeing the horn on the western saddle, and it is a great help to hold on to when you first start riding. Most people find western saddles to be more comfortable for trail riding, but I like my hunt seat saddle best."

The girls carried the saddles and bridles to the stalls where Aubrey proceeded to show Jillian how to put the saddle pad on the horse. "Make sure you start a little above the withers and slide the pad back to the right spot, just here." She showed Jillian how to place the saddle and tighten the girth. It wasn't long before they were leading the horses to the front of the house. Mrs. McKinstry met them at the gate with two helmets.

"You two be careful," she said, handing them their headgear and helping Jillian adjust her chinstrap. "You know the limits of the ride, right Aubrey?" she asked.

"Yup, Mom, I do. We won't go any further than the big meet-up circle before the road crossing. And we won't cross the road, and we won't go through the cholla cactus path. I promise. I have my cell phone, and we already tested the reception, and Zoe and I have ridden this only a hundred million times," she added with a grin.

"You sassy girl," her mom responded with a matching smile. "Now go and have fun and go slow. I know Jillian has ridden several times, but I'll be watching for you. Where is your cell phone?" she asked.

"It's right here, Mom. Don't worry. We're only going to be gone for an hour."

"Okay." Her mom smiled. "Oh, by the way, remember to stay far away from that dog that barks every time, you don't want the horses to spook. It's 11 a.m. right now, so I'll see you at noon. I'll have lunch ready when you get home."

"Sounds good. Thanks, Mom," said Aubrey. She walked Grace up to a two-step mounting block where Mrs. McKinstry held Grace's reins while Aubrey mounted.

"Let me give you a hand too, Jillian." Mrs. McKinstry led Amora to the mounting block. Once Jillian was astride, she asked, "Are you comfortable? Are the stirrups okay in length?" She checked the girth under the saddle to be sure it was snug.

"It feels great, Mrs. McKinstry," replied Jillian. "I wanted to say thanks for letting me ride Amora. She sure is beautiful."

Mrs. McKinstry smiled. "You have a good, safe time. See you for lunch."

The girls pointed their horses toward the climbing desert sun riding side by side down the dirt road.

CHAPTER 12 - A Wild Ride

Jillian was feeling comfortable on Amora as the two girls chattered on their way down to the end of the road. In its wild and desolate way, the desert was beautiful. Pink cacti bloomed along the trail amazing Jillian with their intense color. She'd always thought of the desert as drab sand and scrub and thorny cactus. They crossed a small wash, a dry creek bed, and then Aubrey led them onto a trail off to the right.

"Stay to the far-right side of the trail. There's a dog in the backyard of this last house that likes to bark at the horses. I think it plots to see if the horses can literally jump out of their skins. Anyway, just be careful, and if Amora spooks, just stand up a bit and balance in your stirrups and hold onto the horn. She should be fine though."

The dog did indeed come rushing out, barking like a fiend, but Jillian was ready when Amora skittered sideways with a start.

"Ugh!" cried Aubrey, as Grace gave a little jump and a buck. "Stupid dog. Shut up," she yelled, and she petted Grace's neck to calm her down.

"Loose dogs can be really dangerous to horses." Aubrey had Gracie under control again. "My friend Diana was riding with her mom on the public lands in Cave Creek and there was a lady walking her dog without a leash. The dog rushed up to Diana and bit her gelding on its elbow and tried to grab Diana's leg to pull her out of the saddle. Luckily, her horse is a kicker, and he spun around and kicked at the dog while her mom screamed at the woman. It was horrible."

"Was the horse okay?" asked Jillian, alarmed for Aubrey's friend and thinking how scary it would be to have a loose dog come after her and Amora. She didn't know if she was a good enough rider to stay on a horse that was freaked out. She reached out for the horn in front of her saddle, reassuring herself.

"Yeah, he's okay now, but it took a couple of months to heal, and they're trying to get the owner to pay for their vet bills," answered Aubrey with disgust in her voice. "I don't understand why some people won't take responsibility for their animals."

"I hear you," said Jillian. "It's like the guy with his dad's horses next door to me. You can't just ignore them and hope they'll go away or feed themselves. I wonder if people think animals don't have feelings. I think they do. Speaking of · feelings, I sure hope Lila is okay," added Jillian, changing the subject. "She's so much fun to be around. I really like her. And you," she added with a shy smile at Aubrey.

"Awww." Aubrey shared Jillian's smile. "You're pretty cool yourself."

The trail had two tracks, so they walked side by side. When they reached the road about half an hour into the ride, the sun was blazing down from high in the sky. It was getting hot. As promised, they turned back, but as they were turning, both horses raised their necks, pricked up their ears, and Grace let out an unexpected loud whinny.

"What's that?" asked Jillian, glimpsing movement in the distance. They saw a flash of yellow dashing back and forth. The horses were still staring ahead.

"Let's take a look," suggested Aubrey, and it took very little urging to get the mares to head toward whatever was behind the rise in front of them. They followed a side trail up the small hill, and as they crested the hilltop, what they saw made the horses stop; Jillian felt her stomach tighten in fear.

On the other side of the rise was a gully about thirty feet wide, and on the far side was a steep hill covered in shale and loose stone. At its bottom, a bay mare struggled to free her right hind leg from a pile of rocks. Blood glistened on her leg, and there was a clear trail that marked where she and her baby slid down the hillside in a jumble of stone. Her young foal—unhurt—squealed and skittered back and forth in front of his mother, his eyes wide as he cried out. He had been separated from her in the slide and couldn't get next to her because of all the loose boulders and rocks that had fallen.

The source of his fear lay crouched on a boulder on the hillside just fifteen feet above them twitching its black-tipped, amber tail. As the girls approached, the full-grown mountain lion shifted its golden gaze from the mare and foal to the two girls on horseback; it let out a loud, frustrated yowl. Suddenly, their curious horses were prancing with fear. Jillian was trying hard to calm Amora down.

"We have to get out of here," cried Aubrey. "We can call my mom, but I don't think it is safe to stay here."

"But we can't just leave the mare and foal," replied Jillian, her eyes widening and bright spots of anger coloring her cheeks. "We can't just abandon them. We have to do something. That cat is hunting them. He is going to kill that baby and maybe both of them if we don't do something!"

Jillian was looking around searching for something they could throw at the big cat. She had heard of mountain lions and knew they lived in the Cascade Mountains of Washington, but she had never seen one in person, and she was stunned at its size. It had to be seven feet from the tip of its black nose to the dark tuft on its flicking tail. "What can we do?" she asked Aubrey.

"Okay," Aubrey answered, trying to stay calm. "Let's back up a little bit, and I'll call Mom. Then we can work out a plan to try to keep that lion away from the horses. I'm sure she is going to freak out when I tell her how close to that thing we are."

Jillian felt an instant bond with the terrified foal. If she could do anything to keep that baby and his momma safe, she was going to do it. She kept her gaze on the little foal as they retreated a few paces. With its knobby knees and gangly step, it couldn't be more than a few days old. Amora and Grace had calmed somewhat, but Grace still snorted and Amora stomped in the cat's direction.

"Okay, Mom, yes. We will. We'll be waiting by the road. Please hurry, and bring Dad's gun." Aubrey clicked off her cell phone turning to Jillian. "Mom said we need to leave now and under no circumstances are we to get closer to that mountain lion. We should—"

A scream split the air. It stopped Aubrey and caused the horses to once again prance in fear. The girls stared in horror as the mountain lion flattened itself to the ground and slipped closer to the mare. The horse screamed again wildly trying to free her leg and pinning her ears at the giant feline. Her foal, eyes white with terror, squealed and turned toward the threat; his splayed legs shaking in fear and exhaustion.

Without a thought, Jillian spurred Amora into the gully toward the golden lion. She screamed at the top of her lungs, "Get out! Get out of here! Get out!" and charged the mare toward the hunting cat.

Amora screamed a challenging cry to the cougar and flattened her ears as they neared the mare and foal. Jillian pulled her to a stop a few feet from the mare, and facing the mountain lion, she let out a shriek of anger. At that moment, Jillian didn't feel afraid. She felt mad. Mad at the lion for hurting the mare and threatening the foal. Mad at the unfairness in life, and her feelings of frustration and helplessness. Mad at her parents for leaving her.

The cat screamed its own challenge at the two arching its back and showing its two-inch incisors with a furious hiss. For a moment they stood locked in each other's gaze. The cat's unwavering yellow eyes stared with intensity into the girl's fierce blue glare. They were each unwilling to back down. Just then Amora stomped her foreleg and cried out in defiance baring her own teeth in return.

Jillian—who despite her fierce scowl was close to faltering—gained courage from Amora's actions, and she screamed as loud as she could, "Go away! Get out, cat!"

The lion, startled at the intensity of her scream, turned and scrambled up the rocky hillside in giant leaps leaving Jillian with her heart pounding in her throat.

"What were you thinking," cried Aubrey, as she trotted to Jillian's side. "I mean seriously Jillian, that was really a dumb and totally brave thing to do. Are you okay? Wow! You scared the heck out of me. And you scared the heck out of that mountain lion. Who knew the quiet girl could yell so loud."

Jillian grinned at her friend unable to control her shaking hands as she realized what she had just done. "I don't know what I was thinking. I just didn't want the baby to get hurt. Did you see how awesome Amora was? She was ticked off at that cat. She had her ears all flat back, and she really wanted to chase it away. What a brave girl." Jillian patted the mare's lathered neck appreciating her boldness. If Amora hadn't responded to her urging, the foal would likely be dead.

"I'm going to go back up the rise to get a cell signal and call Mom and have her meet us here. I don't want to leave you alone with the mare and foal, and we can't abandon them now." Aubrey rode up the trail ten or fifteen yards and pulled out her phone.

Meanwhile, Jillian was studying the bay mare and her baby. The mare was a little thin and had burrs and stickers matted into her black mane. A thin white stripe started between her eyes and ran down to her muzzle. The hind leg that was stuck didn't look very good. Jillian didn't think it was broken, but it was hard to see from where she sat on top of Amora.

The foal was a yellow buckskin color with a dark stripe down his back and black on his gangly legs. He had a little spiky dark mane that was adorable. He looked really young as he stood there trembling trying to get as close to his mom as possible.

Jillian wanted to help the mare get free from the stones, but before she could dismount, she heard the roaring sound of a truck climbing the rise. Mrs. McKinstry jumped out, rifle in hand, and went straight to Aubrey who had dismounted. She hugged her close, and then in a cool tone, told them both they would discuss what happened when they got home.

"It was my fault, Mrs. McKinstry. Really it was. Aubrey wanted to go back to the road, but I don't know why, I couldn't let the horses die. I'm sorry. I'm really sorry. Please don't be mad at Aubrey. I am the idiot who ran toward the mountain lion." Jillian felt real remorse at the thought of her friend getting in trouble at her expense.

Mrs. McKinstry's face softened, and she repeated, "We can talk when we get home," but this time it came out with a bit of warmth. "Which way did that cat go?" she asked, and the girls pointed to the top of the hillside. "Jillian, I'd like you to hold the horses, please, while Aubrey and I see what we can do for this mare." She put the rifle on the hood of the truck.

With a rope halter in hand, Mrs. McKinstry spoke softly as she began walking toward the mare. The foal skittered away as she approached, and the mare tried to heave herself out of the rocks. "Whoa, girl. Easy, girl," she murmured to the frightened horse. "Easy, girl. You're okay. I'm going to help you." She kept talking as she approached the mare with an outstretched hand. The mare was scared but seemed to understand they weren't going to hurt her. She stayed still as Mrs. McKinstry reached out to stroke her neck. The frightened mare gave an audible sigh and licked her lips when the rope halter was affixed around her head.

"Aubrey, come here slowly. I want you to hold the mare. Be very careful," she cautioned. Aubrey mimicked her mother's approach walking slowly with eyes cast down and hand outstretched until she reached the mare. The foal stood a few yards away staring at the girl as she took the lead rope from her mom, and Mrs. McKinstry carefully began removing rocks from the pile around the mare.

She made progress until she came to a large, heavy, flat rock. It wouldn't budge. It was too big and heavy for one person to move. The mare had been patient until this point, but she sensed she was close to freedom and she lunged forward yanking Aubrey's arm and pulling on her trapped leg. Instead of moving away, Mrs. McKinstry leaned forward, grabbed the edge of the big rock, and pulled with all her might. Somehow the combined efforts of horse and woman managed to move the rock back just enough for the mare to free her leg with a yank leaving skin and hair behind. Aubrey led her forward a few yards to clear ground where the mare turned nickering for her foal.

"It's okay, girl," Aubrey said. "Here's your baby," and she let the mare stretch out to sniff the colt who had scampered over and was butting her udder looking for milk and comfort. "I wonder how this mare and foal got out here, and who owns them?" Aubrey mused.

"I was thinking the exact same thing," answered Jillian. "I wonder if she was abandoned out here or if she escaped?"

"I'll call the rescue group Healing Horses, which is in Cave Creek, not far away. Hopefully, they'll be able to bring out a trailer and pick them up," Mrs. McKinstry explained. "Let's get the horses out of here and a little closer to the road. We can each lead one and come back for my truck when we're done. We'll have to take it very slowly. That leg needs some tending."

Mrs. McKinstry Googled the rescue and made the call. When she hung up, confirming a trailer was on the way, she locked the rifle in her truck and they started out.

"You should have seen Amora, Mom," declared Aubrey, as they began the short trek to the road. "She was like a war-horse. She ran right toward that thing. She was so brave. You would have been proud to see her," she beamed.

"Well, I'm glad she was brave, but I never, ever want Jillian or you—either of you—to put yourselves into that situation again. Do you understand? Do you know what could have happened to you? Or to Amora?" Mrs. McKinstry scolding the girls. "You scared me to death." Jillian's eyes glistened with guilt.

As they neared the road, a white truck and horse trailer rumbled up in a cloud of dust. Jennifer hopped out of the truck giving Jillian a smile. To Mrs. McKinstry's surprise, she spoke directly to the newcomer. "You sure like to rescue horses don't you, young lady?, "What have we got here?" she asked.

"The girls came across this mare and foal just about a quarter mile from here, up by the hills. Apparently, they slid down a shale slope and the mare got trapped under the rocks.

Her foal is scared but fine. He looks awfully young. I don't think the mare's leg is broken, and she is bearing some weight on it, but it is badly scraped up," Mrs. McKinstry explained. "I arrived about ten minutes after they found the horses, and by then, the mountain lion was gone."

"Mountain lion?" asked Jennifer, furrowing her brow with a look of skepticism.

"Yes. An adult, I understand. This young lady Jillian and my Amora here apparently had the bright idea to chase it off. Lucky for them it worked," Mrs. McKinstry explained.

Jennifer looked at Jillian with a new respect. "Did you really chase a mountain lion?" she asked Jillian.

"Yes, I did, but I didn't think about it, I just... I don't know. I didn't want the horses to get hurt," Jillian trailed off looking at the ground. When she looked up at Jennifer tears were glistening in her eyes. "I just wanted them to be safe and together."

"Well, thanks to you, they will be now." Jennifer gave her an understanding smile. "You're a brave girl," she added, putting her hand on Jillian's shoulder. "Just remember when you are helping horses that you have to stay safe too. I'm proud of you. Three horses in one week." She winked at Jillian.

Mrs. McKinstry looked at Jennifer, puzzled, but Aubrey declared proudly, "My friend is a hero. Don't worry, horses. She's brave. She's strong. She's Jillian to the Rescue!"

Jillian giggled experiencing a wave of warmth as she realized she had actually made a difference in the lives of three animals. She felt happy and good inside. Maybe Arizona wasn't going to be completely awful after all.

CHAPTER 13 - Freedom at Last!

Jillian, Aubrey, and Lila met at Aubrey's house to celebrate their first day of freedom. School was over for the summer. The three girls were getting ready to go on a trail ride in the desert to meet up with some kids from school. The trail ride was an annual event and very popular with the residents of New River, Arizona.

"We need to get going soon." Aubrey urged her friends. "It's already 8 a.m. and the Freedom Ride starts at 9:30. We don't want to miss the beginning. That's my favorite part— seeing all the different horses and riders."

Aubrey was dressed in tan riding breeches, a sleeveless white button-down blouse, black belt, and tall black riding boots. She was crisp and clean and ready to ride. Her long hair was put up in a bun. She looked every bit like she was prepared to go in the show ring. Aubrey gazed out the window at the two horses who were in their enclosures in the backyard. She'd fed and groomed them already impatient for the fun to begin.

"Don't get all worked up yet, Aubs," said Lila, who was expertly twisting her long black hair into its customary knot on top of her head. "We still need to pack the saddlebags with water and snacks. I made some healthy trail cookies last night. They are gluten-free and non-GMO. And they taste awesome." She grinned at her two friends. Her obsession with baking and food was cool with them. She was always making something new or trying a different ingredient and they were her taste testers. Her latest craze was fruit and nut bars.

"I don't know how you don't weigh a million pounds, Lila," teased Jillian. "You look like a beanpole. I mean, a cute beanpole. You know, with freckles," Jillian giggled.

"Hmm, what kind of beans do you think?" replied Lila in a fake-serious voice; her dark smooth-lidded eyes wide open. All three girls started laughing.

"Probably the kind that makes you fart," was Aubrey's retort. They all cracked up at that.

"Do you want me to put up your hair, Jillian?" asked Lila. "I'm pretty good at that too." She grinned a cheesy grin.

"Well, your hair is nice and long and straight and my stupid curly mass won't behave at all. I'll never look cute with my hair up 'cause it never, ever stays." Jillian's bright red curls bounced around her head ignoring her futile attempts to gather them into a rubber band.

"Here. Look, I can do it," repeated Lila, as she stood behind Jillian. "Now just hold still." She tugged and twisted and clipped Jillian's curls. "See," she beamed. "It's all set. Take a look in the mirror." Jillian's hair was somehow constrained in a little bun. With wispy red tendrils on either side of her cheeks, her bright blue eyes seemed huge in her white, freckled face.

"Very pretty, if I say so myself," exclaimed Lila, grinning at Jillian's reflection. "Trace is going to like it," she added.

"Shut up, Beanpole," responded Jillian, pushing Lila on her shoulder. Her jeans were tucked into a brand-new pair of simple leather cowboy boots her grandma had given her as a surprise to wear on the ride. She wore one of her favorite plain army-green t-shirts.

"You girls get packed and get going," called Mrs. McKinstry. "And no adventures on the way, okay? Promise?" she said, looking at Jillian who blushed under her gaze. "And be careful during the ride too. Amora doesn't like getting too close to other horses, so make sure to keep a respectful distance. Okay?"

"Okay, I promise," replied Jillian.

"Us too. We promise," added Aubrey.

"Get the extra helmet out of the closet for Lila. You are going to ride one of the ranch horses, Lila. Is that right?"

"It sure is, Mrs. McKinstry. A cow horse. Just in case we run into any wild cattle," Lila joked.

"Well, you stay away from wild cattle too. And snakes. And especially mountain lions," she added, looking at Jillian again.

By then everyone knew about Jillian's little adventure. It seemed odd that it was only last weekend the two girls had their encounter with the mountain lion and loose mare and foal. The story of Jillian's bravery for chasing the big cat away from the horses had been applauded in school, and even Whitney and her gang of bullies had stopped calling her "Clownface."

But only a few people knew about the young Arabian mare that had been abandoned in the vacant property just up the road from her grandma's house. After telling Aubrey on the day of the mountain lion encounter, Jillian had told Lila on Monday. She still hadn't breathed a word to her grandmother about Jamila.

She was going to tell her grandma last weekend, but when she got home from their adventurous ride and Aubrey's mom told Grandma Allison what happened, her grandma almost made her stop riding altogether. She didn't want to rock the boat right now. And she still didn't technically own the horse or anything. She would tell her grandma... soon.

Jillian felt a pang of loss. It was now a familiar feeling. She missed her parents today more than ever. They would have let her keep the horse. She was sure of it. Well, pretty sure of it. Her parents liked horses. Of course, if they were alive, she wouldn't be here in Arizona and would never have saved Jamila in the first place. If they hadn't died… The thought made her sad.

Jillian didn't realize how sad she must have looked until Lila and Aubrey both gave her a quick hug. She hugged them back and wiped her eyes.

"Let's get this show on the road," Lila exclaimed, stuffing the last of the trail bars into the saddlebags. "Ouch! What the heck?" She jerked her hand back to see a pinprick of blood on her index finger.

"Oh, sorry. My bad," said Aubrey. "That's the fine comb we use for getting burrs or stickers off the horses. Believe me, if one of our horses gets stuck by a cholla or any other cactus, you'll be really glad we have that. Just put it in the other pocket. Thanks." Lila rearranged the bags, and they headed out to the horses.

Grace whinnied to them as they took the stairs past the pool down to the back of the property.

"I already groomed them, so we just have to get them saddled up, and we can go. I even lunged Grace this morning, and I'm super glad I did. She was a nut!" Aubrey laughed as Grace nodded her head up and down. "Yeah, you agree, huh?"

Just as they had last weekend, Aubrey carried the heavy western saddle for Jillian and hiked it up onto Amora's back. She reminded Jillian how to tighten the girth that went under her belly.

"You want to make sure it's snug, but if you pull up super-fast, it irritates her. Sometimes Grace will hold her breath so when I think it's tight, it really isn't. I always double-check before I mount. Make sure you check again when we get up the driveway."

"Aye, aye, captain!" saluted Jillian, standing at attention.

"Haha. Hilarious." Aubrey rolled her eyes with a smile on her face.

"You are kind of like the captain you know, Aubs. I mean, around horses anyway. You know, you're kind of bossy. And in school. You are the smartest girl going into eighth grade," exclaimed Lila

"Don't talk about school. We just got out. We have a whole summer before we need to think about eighth grade. Here, make yourself useful and help me with Grace," she admonished Lila, acting very captain-like.

They went through the gate at the top of the driveway where Mrs. McKinstry was holding up their saddlebags.

"You might want these." She held them out with a smile. "I don't think Lila could make it through the day without them."

"Thank you, Mrs. McKinstry," Lila answered with a grin. "One of you has to carry them since I'm not riding yet."

"They can go on Amora. She's used to carrying them," Mrs. McKinstry said, helping Jillian adjust them to fit snugly just in front of the saddle. She checked Amora's girth and pulled it a bit tighter, then led the horse forward so Jillian could use the mounting block.

"Thanks, Mrs. McKinstry. And thanks for letting me ride Amora again. I promise not to chase any wild animals." Jillian smiled down at her friend's mom.

She tried not to feel jealous of Aubrey. She was happy for her friend who had parents who spent time with her and listened to her. She had been trying hard not to let sad thoughts of her mom and dad creep in when she was with her friends. It would be so much worse if she didn't have Aubrey and Lila to help her adjust to her new life. She only wished her parents could see her riding in the desert. They would be proud.

Jillian let a single tear leak from her eye before gathering the reins and shaking it off. She was not going to ruin the fun for her friends. And Trace was going to be there. She was happy and oddly nervous to see him.

Aubrey led the way, and Lila brought up the rear of their procession as they headed to the big trail ride.

CHAPTER 14 - Unhappy Trails

The three girls walked down to the end of Lazy G Road. Instead of turning right like they had the previous weekend, Aubrey led them to the left down a long dirt driveway. At the end of the drive, there was a path through the desert to the ranch that Jillian could see about a quarter of a mile away.

"Wow, you weren't kidding. The ranch is close by." Jillian's butterflies started flapping in her stomach. She was nervous to ride around Trace. She knew she wasn't a great rider since she hadn't taken any lessons. She hoped he didn't expect her to go galloping down the trail.

"Close by? That's not close. Close is, like, next door. You want me to walk on foot through that desert?" Lila complained. "What about snakes, huh? Or scorpions?"

"Here. Quit whining. Come here and climb up on this rock. I've taken Zoe double before. Just climb on behind me carefully. And then you can hold on to my waist." Aubrey positioned Grace so that she was to the right of a large rock. Lila stood on the rock and tried to reach her leg up over Grace's back. She was too short to reach.

"We need a bigger rock." Lila jumped down and scouted the area. "There, just across the trail, over there by that fence. See the stone wall. Can you get her next to that?" she asked Aubrey, picking her way through the sage brush to the wall. Lila was about to climb up when a hare—a desert hare with huge ears and long legs—burst out of the scrub at the bottom of the wall.

Grace snorted and jumped sideways, spinning around and crashing into Amora who staggered to stay upright. Jillian felt herself falling sideways, and she grabbed for the horn, but it was too late. She couldn't grasp it in time, and she fell hard on her back to the ground with a 'thunk.'

"Oh my gosh, are you okay?" Lila cried. "I'm so sorry!"

"Grab Amora's reins, Lila," Aubrey said, as she dismounted. "Thanks. Now hand them to me." Turning to Jillian, who was sitting up and taking off her helmet, she asked, "Are you alright? It looked like you hit your head pretty good. Do you feel dizzy? Are you okay?"

"Yeah, I think I'm okay." Jillian was rubbing the back of her head. She was glad she had been wearing a helmet. She didn't want to think of what might have happened if she hadn't. There was a small bump on her head, and her elbows were scraped up a bit.

Jillian started to get up and Lila jumped to her side to help.

"Really, I'm sorry. I didn't even think about rabbits jumping out of the brush. Are you okay?" she asked Jillian again.

"I'm okay," said Jillian, brushing off her arms and jeans. "But you wrecked my hair," she added with a little jab that made Lila smile.

"Well, stand still, and I'll fix it." She stepped behind Jillian and did some twisting and rubber-banding. "Here you go. Now, all done and perfect again." Lila helped her put her helmet back on.

"Thanks. Now, let's get back on and get to the ranch. And thank goodness I fell off here in front you and not anyone else," Jillian added.

This time there was no fuss. Aubrey gave Jillian a leg up onto Amora and then mounted Grace from the ground, her long leg easily reaching the stirrup,. She guided Grace to the wall and Lila was able to scoot on behind her. Lila grabbed Aubrey's waist and they started down the trail.

There were already rows of trailers and at least thirty or more people milling around the front of the ranch. Some were on horseback and some were getting tacked up. Almost half of them were kids from school. It amazed Jillian to see how many people around here had horses. In Woodinville, there were some barns and a few kids she'd grown up with had horses. It wasn't like here. It seemed like more than half of the kids in school had horses of their own. Aubrey waved to some friends who were eating doughnuts next to a table with coffee and milk and a package of Krispy Kremes. She guided Grace over to see them.

Jillian spied Trace standing next to the big outdoor riding arena, his curly brown hair covering his eyes as he helped someone adjust their saddle. She couldn't see who he was with until he took the reins to hold the horse as its rider walked to the left side of the horse and mounted. Like Aubrey, Whitney was dressed in English hunt seat clothes: tan breeches, a sky-blue sleeveless top, and knee-high boots. Her steel grey horse was huge and looked expensive. She swung her leg across the horse's back, settling into the saddle gracefully, and finding her stirrups. Jillian saw a flash of blonde hair a second before she heard a trill of laughter, and she watched Whitney lean down to say something to Trace. Her perfectly coiffed golden hair was tucked into a velvet riding helmet, and her gloved hand cupped over his ear as if to share a secret.

Jillian's stomach turned sour. She knew Whitney had been trying to get Trace to pay attention to her most of the year. How could he not pay attention? She was pretty and rich. Not very nice, but how much did that matter to Trace? She stopped Amora, wondering if this ride was a good idea.

Jillian felt like she had back in Woodinville on the day after her parent's death. It felt like she was shrouded in an invisible cocoon. Wrapped tightly in her pain and grief, she had felt more alone in the crowd of friends who came to visit her than she'd ever felt before. She remembered feeling piercing loneliness. Even now, with Lila and Aubrey, she sometimes felt alone. And often with Grandma Allison. She had no strong connection to anyone. Except maybe Jamila. Tears flowed unnoticed, and she turned Amora away deciding she would just ride home.

"Hey, Jillian!" She heard Trace's voice calling her. She took a deep breath and turned back seeing the boy jog toward her. He had put on a white cowboy hat, and he looked every bit the part with his boots, jeans, and plaid short-sleeved shirt. His green eyes searched her face.

"Hi, Trace," she said, avoiding eye contact. "I see you're busy. I don't feel very well for some reason. Maybe I should just go home." She faltered struggling to keep from crying. It wasn't just that a silly boy would rather like a pretty girl who happened to be a bully; her whole life situation was breaking her heart.

"Wait. What's the matter? What happened? And no, I'm not busy, I was just helping that girl Whitney with her girth. I swear that she knows how to do it but plays helpless just to keep me occupied."

"Girls who act like that can be a pain, can't they?" Jillian observed. "Never mind, I'm okay. I better go find Aubrey." Changing the subject, she added, "Isn't Lila borrowing a horse from you?" Jillian turned Amora once again and urged her forward not wanting to talk to Trace or to anyone until she had her emotions under control.

The ride got started fifteen minutes later. Jillian had found Aubrey, and although she was still feeling glum, she wasn't on the verge of tears anymore. It was weird like that. Sometimes grief would wash over her like a giant wave of sadness and loneliness, and after it crested, she was left feeling empty and tired.

"Don't you like my cool ride?" Lila rode her chestnut quarter horse up next to Jillian. "This hare's a trayned cow horse. He happens ta be naymed Tex," she said with a Texan drawl. "Me an' this horse here, we're gonna rahd off into the desert and find us some cattle, raght boy?" She leaned down and patted the gelding's neck.

"Okay, Tex," mimicked Jillian. "You gonna show us how it's done," she added, playing along. "That there's a maghty fian animal. Maghty fian."

All three girls started laughing as they carried on talking with southern drawls. Jillian was once again grateful for her friends who helped her out of her black moods. At least she had some friends and she was learning to ride and Jamila was getting better every day. She made a concerted effort to think positively. It was the only thing she could do.

Riding in a wide, sandy wash, the trail riders spread out in groups of two to six. Jillian hadn't seen Trace or Whitney since their interaction at the arena. She and Lila were talking about the trail bars, which Lila insisted she try even though they weren't ten minutes into the ride.

"They're good. Really. You have to try one," she encouraged Jillian.

"But I don't want one now. I'm not hungry. Why do you want me to eat one right now?" Jillian said, shaking her head.

"I just want your opinion. I think they are amazing, but I want you to let me know what you think," insisted Lila.

"Just take a bite of a cookie, Jillian, or I swear she won't stop bugging you. They are probably delicious. Her cookies usually are," Aubrey advised.

"Okay. Fine." Jillian reached into the saddlebag and brought out a Ziploc bag of trail bars or cookies or whatever they were. She broke off a piece and shoved it into her mouth. She searched her bag for a bottle of water. The bar was dry and her mouth was full of oats and raisins. But it did taste good, she thought, her mouth still stuffed.

Just then Whitney trotted by on her big grey gelding looking like Miss Put Together. She spied Jillian with her cheeks bulging and laughed out loud before trotting off to join her friends. Jillian turned red. She choked down the last of the bite and took a swig of water.

"Uh, sorry about that," apologized Lila. "I mean, how was I supposed to know that the Queen of Mean was going to ride by right then? Think about it this way, at least it wasn't Trace who saw you stuff your face."

"Are you talking about me? Stuff your face with what?" Trace rode up alongside.

"Ah, nothing, Trace. Nothing. Jillian was just taste testing my latest creation. Do you want to try a trail bar that I made? It's non-GMO," Lila gushed, trying to deflect. "Well, I'd um, better go look for some cows now." She urged her horse forward with a twinkle in her dark brown eyes, leaving Trace and Jillian riding side by side.

Jillian couldn't help but admire his horse. The black gelding was big bodied and at least five inches taller than Amora. His only white was a thin, crooked stripe down his face and one white sock that came up to his left hind ankle. Trace rode him in a beat-up western saddle that had a breast strap and a second belly strap in the back. Curious, she couldn't help but ask about the second strap. It was snug but not tight at all. Before he could speak first, Jillian asked, "What is that strap for? I haven't seen one before."

"Oh, it's called a 'back cinch,' and it's connected to the front cinch to make sure the saddle doesn't slide. Mostly they are used when roping or doing ranch work. It keeps my saddle where it belongs when a steer is at the other end of the rope.

"Hey, Jillian, I hope you're okay. Did I say something or do something stupid?" he asked, with earnest eyes under the coffee colored curls that peeked out from under his cowboy hat.

Jillian hadn't spoken to Trace about her parents very much. Like the rest of the kids in school, he knew she had moved her to live with her grandma, and he'd heard her parents were dead. They hadn't spent enough time together for her to share the pain she was feeling. She wasn't even sure he was interested in getting to know her.

"No. You didn't do anything. It's me. I've been in kind of a bad mood. But I don't want it to spoil the ride." Jillian avoided adding details and Trace seemed to accept her answer.

"Any time you want to talk, just let me know, okay?" he responded as if he could sense the tenderness of the topic. He smiled at her with an honest smile, and Jillian felt silly she had ever doubted his motives.

"What is your horse's name and how old is he?" Jillian asked, looking for a safe topic.

"His name is Ted. I know, it's kind of a funny name. His registered name is Teddy Got His Guns, which is also kind of a silly name. His grandfather was a champion cow horse. He's only four, so he's still kind of green."

"Hate to break it to you, dude, but he's black, not green," Jillian quipped

"Ha, ha." His eyes twinkled "'Green' means fresh or new at something. A green horse is one that is just started and still learning."

"Oh, okay. So, I guess Jamila is green." The last part slipped out before she realized what she was saying.

"Who is Jamila? Is that a horse?"

"Ahh, well, I guess, um, yes." Jillian decided to tell Trace about the horse she rescued that was living next door. "Yes," she repeated, and she recounted the story of finding the starved horse under a tumbled down shelter.

Trace listened to her tale and seemed impressed by her selfless actions. Neither of them realized they had become separated from the rest of the riders. They continued on down the wash talking about horses and the different breeds. Jillian was eager to learn more about horses and Trace was happy to share his experiences.

"So you are telling me that the Arabian is the oldest breed of horses? How do you know about Arabians?" Jillian asked.

"Yup," Trace answered. "They were prized for their abilities in endurance and the Bedouins of the desert called them 'Drinkers of the Wind,'" he added. "My dad and uncle raised Arabians for a while when I was young. He had a stallion that was by Bey Shah, a famous—"

"Help!"

Jillian and Trace pulled their horses to a stop. Listening.

"Help me!" It was a girl.

"Hang on! We're coming," answered Trace, as he and Jillian trotted up the side of the wash to the desert above.

Frozen on a giant cholla cactus, they spotted Whitney's grey gelding. The cactus was stuck to his front legs and under his belly. Unable to dismount without landing in more cactus, and with the back of her shirt snared, Whitney was stuck and panicking. Her horse stood still like a champ, clearly more sensible than his rider.

CHAPTER 15 - A Sticky Situation

Jillian almost burst out laughing. With her blotchy, red face, her tangled hair, and the large rip she had made in the back of her shirt attempting to free herself, Whitney looked hilarious. But Jillian also felt empathy for the girl, and she swallowed back the bark of laughter that threatened to escape.

"How the heck did you get up here? And stuck like that?" Trace sounded a little annoyed.

"Well, I didn't mean to get stuck, of course!" Whitney's face reddened again. "I saw something. I'm pretty sure it was a wild horse. I wanted to make sure it wasn't stuck or hurt," she continued. "So I rode Aragon up here, and when I saw it was nothing, I turned him to go down the wash and there was a snake." Her blue eyes widened at the memory. "I tried to back him up, and then we slipped and got stuck. Thank God the snake took off. I've been here calling forever. Where is everyone?" Her gratitude at their arrival turned to whining. "Well, don't just stand there. Get me out of here," Whitney demanded.

"That's easy to say. You must have figured out that if you move around, the spines will just go in deeper. I don't think Aragon can take much more. You need to stay still. We won't be able to clear these without a sickle or blade of some kind." Trace thought for a moment trying to determine the quickest way to free the pair.

"Okay, I have an idea. Jillian," he said turning to her, "can you get off of your horse and stay here with Whitney? I'll go back to the house and get a tool and some help to get her out. Do either of you have a cell phone?"

"If I had a cell phone, I wouldn't still be stuck here, Trace," Whitney said with vehemence. "I'd have called someone who knew what to do long ago. But, if this is your plan, then you'd better get going. I don't know how long Aragon is going to stay still, and I've been here long enough."

Trace shook his head at her attitude but said nothing. He wheeled Ted around and galloped off. Jillian stared after him. *Geez, that was just like in the movies*, she thought watching him ride off on his black horse with his white cowboy hat.

Jillian dismounted and walked around the cactus patch that held Whitney prisoner. The plants were between five and eight feet tall. Their brown, spiky trunks split into multiple branches that from a distance appeared to be covered in a whitish fuzz. Upon closer inspection, the "fuzz" was made of zillions of thorns that stuck out in all directions. She had learned from Aubrey the ends of the needles were hooked and would burrow deeper as their host moved about.

Jillian, careful not to let Amora near any of the cactus, picked her way around Whitney looking for an easy way out. There wasn't one. The only thing they could do was cut back the cactus that they'd gotten stuck behind. Then they would still have to free Aragon.

"Ouch!" Whitney cried, trying to arch her back away from the prickers that were working their way into her shoulder. She was in real pain and though she tried to hold back, Jillian saw fresh tears slide down her cheek and she remembered something.

"I don't know if you can catch it, but if you can, this might help," she said, looking into the saddlebag to find the fine-toothed comb Aubrey had insisted on. "I'm going to have to toss it to you. Don't lean too far or Aragon might move. And we only have one shot at this, so please catch it."

"Of course, I'll catch it," snapped Whitney, holding out her hands.

Jillian got as close as she could to Aragon and Whitney. There was a big cholla between them and she would have to lob the comb up and over the plant. She paused to steady herself hoping she wouldn't miss.

"Hurry up," insisted Whitney.

"Okay, here you go," and Jillian threw the comb over the cactus. Whitney reached out with both hands and caught it. She almost dropped it when the fine tines hit her hands, but she held on. She stretched her arm backward to the middle of her shoulders and was able to just reach the ball of thorns. She managed to get the tines through the thorns and jerked the comb sending the glob of spines flying.

"Owwww! That hurt!" Whitney jerked in the saddle slumping forward. Blood trickled down her back staining her blue blouse in purple streaks.

Jillian saw Aragon shift and tense. "Please try to stay still. Aragon looks like he is about to lose it." The big horse let out a loud whinny that surprised and frightened both girls. If he started to move now, they would only get more entangled.

"Whoa, boy. Whoa. It's okay, baby," Whitney crooned stroking his neck to calm him. Aragon responded, letting out a big sigh.

Jillian couldn't help but be impressed by the relationship between the blond girl and her horse. The Mean Girl from school communicated with Aragon with a kindness that she rarely showed people. Jillian decided it was time to be blunt with her.

"I have a question for you," Jillian began.

Whitney looked down at her, "Well, what is it?"

"Why do you hate me?" Jillian asked looking at her directly.

Whitney raised her chin defiantly. "I don't hate you. I just don't like you. There's a difference."

"I still don't get it. Why do you have to pick on me? I didn't do anything to you. I just don't know why you and your gang make fun of me." Jillian had her hands on her hips.

"I don't know why exactly," she responded tersely. "You just showed up and made friends on the first day and now Trace likes you and... whatever."

Jillian looked at Whitney seeing her differently for the first time. She realized Whitney was jealous of her. That was surprising. Why would she be jealous of an orphan? "When did you and your family move to Anthem?" Jillian asked. "I thought you'd lived here for a long time. You seem to have friends."

"I live on the golf course with my mother. Well, when she decides to come home. She has a busy life, you know, spending my dad's money. We moved here a year ago. I hate it." She spat the last three words.

Jillian understood that sentiment. She'd felt the same when she first moved here. It surprised her she had something in common with Whitney. She struggled to imagine her mom not wanting to spend time with her. Jillian felt sorry for the beautiful girl. She was at a loss as to what to say next, but soon they were interrupted.

"Hey, Jillian! Whitney! I've got help on the way," called Trace, as he loped his big black horse toward the girls. They could hear the rev of an engine as a red Jeep crested the side of the wash. Trace had found his father at the ranch, and they'd come equipped to cut or drag the cholla away from the girl and her horse.

Jillian could see where Trace got his curly hair. His dad, tall and slender in jeans and a white t-shirt, had dark brown curls flipping up behind the back of his ball cap. He smiled at her when she neared the jeep with Amora in hand. "Looks like you two managed to keep the horse from freaking out. Good job."

Whitney had regained her composure and her unpleasant tongue. "Can we please just get me out of here!"

Mr. Carter plucked a length of rope from the back of the Jeep along with a long, wooden fruit picking device. "We're gonna do just that, young lady. Just try to be patient. The calmer you are, the easier it'll be for your horse to stay still.

"Trace, stand over on the other side of the cactus. I'll use the picker to push the rope past the cholla so you can grab it. Make sure you have your gloves on." Trace pulled on a pair of heavy leather gloves, and father and son approached the cholla that kept the horse and girl trapped. Mr. Carter made a knot at the end of the rope and placed it in the metal tines of the fruit picker. The end looked almost like a spider with prongs bent out and then back to the center. He pushed the pole through the back of the cactus. It got snagged several times, but at last, Trace was able to reach out and take hold of the knot and pass it around the trunk of the cactus and back to his father.

His dad tied a slipknot at the end, and slid it until it was snug around the trunk of the cactus. Reaching his Jeep, he tied the other end of the rope to the rear bumper, and said, "Now try to hold your horse still until there is a clear path. He's probably not going to like it when the cactus starts moving. Try to keep him in control if you can.

"Trace, I want you to be ready to grab the reins, and Jillian, let's make sure your horse is out of the way. Can you take her close to the wash so she doesn't get spooked?" Jillian complied. Mr. Carter got in the Jeep and put it into gear. He slowly drove forward until the rope was taut. Then he gunned the engine to gain torque, and the cholla leaned away from Whitney.

There was a loud "pop!" and the roots exploded from the ground. Aragon, unable to keep it together any longer and having endured the pain of the cactus embedded in his belly and leg, spun toward the opening and leaped over the exposed roots. Trace lunged toward the frightened horse and was able to get hold of the reins. Whitney jumped off, bending to examine the stickers that were attached to her frightened animal. She hugged him with relief, murmuring soothing words to calm him down.

"Are you okay?" Mr. Carter saw the blood on Whitney's back. "We better get you cleaned up. I brought the first aid kit."

"Not until Aragon is okay. Jillian gave me this comb. I can keep him calm if you can take them out for me." She handed Mr. Carter the small comb and stood by Aragon's head stroking his face and talking softly to him. The horse was in pain, jerking each time they removed a spine, and getting the cholla out was difficult. Finally, after twenty minutes the big grey was free of barbs and his bleeding wounds were swiped with antibiotic cream.

Whitney turned to Jillian and Trace. "Thanks for helping. I, um, well, you know, appreciate it and all." Her awkwardness made it clear she wasn't used to saying thank you. But it was a start.

CHAPTER 16 - Truth Be Told

Aubrey and Lila were waiting in the wash for Jillian and Trace to join them. They had heard that there was an adventure going on and were dying to find out what happened. Both were anxious to know Jillian was okay and to hear the scoop first hand.

"Finally! We were worried. What the heck happened up there?" Lila demanded as soon as Jillian arrived. "Are you okay?"

"Is Amora okay?" asked Aubrey, looking concerned.

"I'm fine. Amora is fine. Trace will be here in a sec with Aragon." Seeing the confusion on her friends' faces, Jillian added, "Whitney and her horse, Aragon, got stuck in some cholla. Trace raced back to the ranch while I stayed with Whitney. Mr. Carter brought the Jeep and he dragged the cholla out of the way so they could get out. He's driving Whitney home to take care of her cuts—she got some nasty scratches on her back—and Trace is going to bring Aragon back with us." She didn't say anything about what she learned about Whitney.

Trace arrived riding Ted and leading Aragon. The grey gelding was limping, and blood was seeping from the injuries on his leg and belly. Amora and Grace nickered to him with encouragement, and that seemed to bolster the gelding giving him just a little more spring in his step.

"Wow. So you two had to save Whitney? How was that?" Ever curious Lila wanted to know more. Trace looked at Jillian and she smiled.

"Let's just say that she wasn't totally polite about it," responded Trace. "At least not in the beginning. I gotta give her props for how much she cares for Aragon though. She was really worried about him. He was a champ too, standing still for so long."

Aubrey snorted. "Sheesh, there is no way that Grace would stand for more than a minute. If it had been us, we'd still be in there getting deeper and deeper into trouble. Do you know what breed Aragon is? He sure is beautiful."

"I think she said he's a Dutch Warmblood. She's had him for three years, and she told me he is twelve years old. He's what they call a 'schoolmaster.' That's a horse that is very well trained, and its knowledge of advanced moves in dressage help his rider to feel what it is supposed to feel like when a dressage move is done correctly." Trace directed his answer at Jillian who knew very little about dressage.

"That's exactly right," Aubrey agreed. "Dressage riding is centered on a connection between horse and rider, and the moves are very precise. It isn't easy. During tests, you get marked down if your circles aren't perfect or your horse isn't relaxed or for any little mistake. I took dressage lessons for a few months last year. I rode a schoolmaster in my lessons, and it was so cool." Her eyes lit up. "When I was learning how to do a side pass—that's when the horse's front and back legs cross over each other so you move sideways—I could feel my horse's response so that I got used to it. I'm training Grace to side pass now, and it helps because I know how it is supposed to feel."

"I bet a horse like Aragon cost plenty of bucks," Lila speculated. "I wonder how much he is worth."

"I wouldn't be surprised if he'd cost tens of thousands of dollars," answered Aubrey.

"Whoa! No way," Jillian exclaimed, completely surprised by the price. "People pay that much for horses?" She had a hard time believing anyone would spend as much money on a horse as they might on a car.

"Oh, sure they do. Warmbloods and hunter/jumpers and breeds like Friesians can easily be in the twenty- to fifty-thousand-dollar range. The very best can cost more than $100,000. I mean, heck, racehorses sell for millions." Aubrey explained.

"Wouldn't it be cool to breed a horse and have a million-dollar baby?" Lila got excited at the idea. "We could breed it every year and make a million dollars a year. Just from one horse. Oh, yeah, that's what I'm talking about!"

Aubrey shook her head at her goofy friend. "First of all, if you want to breed a million-dollar baby, you need a very well-bred mare. And a well-known stallion who has proven to cross just right with her breeding. You could pay, I don't know, five thousand, maybe ten thousand dollars for the breeding. Then there are vet bills and ultrasounds and shots and foaling. It isn't cheap. Even then you could breed the same two horses together and they might produce a champion one year, and a dud the next. Breeding is risky. That's what my mom says. That's why we haven't bred Amora. She is a nice mare and has a good pedigree, but it would be hard to sell her baby for very much unless it somehow turned out to be incredible. More likely she would have a nice baby, but nothing super special. A million dollars is great, but not easy to make."

"Burst my bubble. Wah!" Lila stuck her tongue out at Aubrey. "You're always so practical. You gotta dream a little, Aubs!"

"I dream plenty of dreams. Just not dumb ones that don't make sense," Aubrey retorted. "Anyway, unless you have fifty thousand or so in your savings account to buy a mare and breed her, then this is a silly conversation."

"I like silly conversations. They're fun." Lila had them all giggling all the way back to the ranch.

Jillian got home that afternoon happy and a little sore from the long ride. Her legs were like jelly. She felt weak, but it was that good feeling she got when she exercised. She entered the kitchen trying not to let the screen door slam behind her. Grandma Allison and Aaron were sitting at the dining room table.

"Hi, Grandma! I had a great ride. And no mountain lions this time." She grinned at her grandmother. "Whitney got stuck in some cactus, but we got her out. The ride was so much fun." She babbled on about the ride, getting a glass out of the white cupboard and pouring herself some milk. She took it to the dining table and sat down with them, searching her grandma's face. "What's wrong?"

Grandma Allison looked at Aaron and then back at her. "Do you have anything you want to tell me about, Jillian?" she asked, looking at her granddaughter.

"I don't know what you mean, Grandma…" Jillian trailed off. She glanced at Aaron. He wore a smirk on his face. Her heart dropped to her stomach and her face flushed. She knew that somehow, they had learned about Jamila. She'd been meaning to tell her grandma about the horse, but the time never seemed right, and she was afraid her grandmother wouldn't let her keep the mare. She regretted she had lied by omission, and she had the good sense to feel ashamed.

"You know exactly what she's talking 'bout, don't you?" Aaron's voice was mocking. "Tell her about that little horse you have stashed next door. Tell her how much money they cost and how expensive they are to feed and take care of. Go ahead, tell her you want to adopt her and pay good money to feed her.

We can't afford a horse and you know it!" Aaron unloosed his pent-up anger until he was yelling. His face had flushed, and the bitterness and resentment that shone in his eyes sent Jillian back in her chair.

"Let Jillian tell me about it, Aaron," Grandma Allison said. She looked sad and Jillian knew she was the cause. It made it all worse.

"I'm so sorry, Grandma," Jillian's face fell as she finally told the truth. "I didn't mean to find her. Remember when Aaron told me they were getting rid of some horses at Hank's place, and I watched them take the horses away? Well, I was just sitting there after they left when I heard something. I had no idea there was a horse left there. She was underneath a corrugated roof that had fallen down on her. Grandma, please believe me. I planned to tell you. I've wanted to tell you since that day. She is at Bill's house. Her name is Jamila. She is an Arabian horse, and she is so beautiful."

Aaron said, "And you wanna pay to adopt her and take care of her. We barely have enough money to live decently, and now that we finally get some luck and get two grand a month so our lives are better, and you want to spend it on a horse? That is just stupid. And not fair. We're your family, you know."

Jillian hadn't thought of it that way before. Maybe Aaron was right and she was being selfish. But the thought of losing Jamila was too awful and she spoke out. "I just couldn't leave her there to starve. And she is getting better every day. Grandma, can you please come and meet her? She's so sweet and friendly; I know you'll love her. Bill said she can stay at his house and he'll even help me. Please, Grandma, please—she's all alone like me." Her eyes filled with fear and sadness.

"I know Jennifer from the rescue will give me a fair deal," Jillian said. "And I do have four hundred dollars per month that my parents wanted me to have to spend on what I want." Her chin lifted a little with the last few words. It was true. She'd read the letter herself.

Aaron snorted in disgust, but his mother answered, "Well, it can't hurt to go and meet the horse. I really don't know anything about horses though." She frowned, looking uncertain.

"No, none of us know anything about horses," insisted Aaron. "That's why it's a stupid idea."

"Now, Aaron." Allison looked at her son sharply. She knew he wanted to use all of Jillian's inheritance to live on so he wouldn't have to work. He'd practically said so himself last week. "Jillian is right. She has her own spending money, and it's what your sister wanted. If she wants to spend the money on a horse, if it is reasonable and it makes Jillian happy here in Arizona, I'm going to at least consider it. But if it is going to end up costing us too much, then we won't be able to keep her. So no more calling anything or anyone stupid." She ended with a glare at Aaron.

"Thank you, Grandma. Thanks so much!" Jillian felt her tense shoulders relax, relieved that the secret was now out. "We can go see her right now if you want. She's right next door." Jumping up from the table, Jillian was excited to introduce Jamila to her grandma.

Aaron scowled and stomped out of the house slamming the back door. He was furious at Jillian for so many reasons: She had only been in Arizona for a little over a month, and she was already his mother's favorite. She didn't do a thing to help pay for anything, so if she got money from his dead sister, then it should be family money. He deserved a better life than working every day, getting yelled at by contractors, and never having enough money to have fun. When he'd learned of her inheritance, he thought it was a way to make his life easier. But no, she wanted to spend it all on a dumb horse. Aaron sat on the short wall that surrounded their backyard glaring in the direction of Bill's house.

Jillian burst out of the back door smiling and followed by his mother.

"Are you coming with us?" his mother asked.

"I don't want to see a stupid creature that is going to take food out of our mouths. No. I still think it is a big mistake."

"Very well." And they set off up the drive with Jillian holding his mother's hand skipping like a little kid.

Aaron was determined to find a way to keep Jillian from adopting that horse. He'd think of something. He would find a way to prove how expensive those animals could be. He thought of different ways to make his point until a slow smile appeared on his conniving face. He began to formulate his plan.

CHAPTER 17 - Introductions

Jillian and her grandmother first knocked on Bill's front door. Ordinarily, Jillian would have gone straight to visit Jamila, but her grandma insisted they let Bill know they were there.

Bill swung open the door, his huge frame filling the doorway. He was dressed as he often was in jeans, work boots, and a t-shirt. His bushy red beard covered his round face and wiry eyebrows sheltered kind, blue eyes.

"Hello, Mrs. Parker. What a pleasure ta see ya here," he said. He winked at Jillian knowing she had been struggling to tell her grandmother about the horse.

"Hello, Bill," Allison said warmly. "It's been too long since we've visited. Heavens, you're just next door, and it seems silly that I haven't seen you in months."

"You're right. It does seem silly. We'll have ta change that," he affirmed. "But yer granddaughter here's been stoppin' by regular. I'm real glad that she told ya 'bout Jamila. She's a real sweet horse. Jillian was very brave ta save 'er an' the two are quite the pair now."

"Can't we go see her now?" interrupted Jillian, unable to contain her excitement.

Bill laughed and said, "Ya can see she's mighty enthusiastic about the horse. Come on back an' meet 'er."

They walked down the flagstone path that meandered through Bill's lush yard where rich colors edged the brilliant green of his manicured lawn. Through the side gate and just past the garage door stood a metal-roofed open barn that contained two stalls with pole fencing.

Jamila greeted Jillian with a whinny and a toss of her head. She was still thin and had a long way—several hundred pounds—to get to a healthy weight. Every rib could be counted, her neck seemed too thin to carry her head despite a delicate face that started with a tiny muzzle and widened to huge liquid eyes. Her hipbones showed although her skin was no longer stretched tight across them. She had been bathed and groomed so that her golden mane was no longer matted with burrs and bits of cactus; however, it was still short and the hair in poor condition.

Allison couldn't hide her gasp at the condition of the horse. Seeing Jamila for the first time was shocking to a gentle-hearted soul. She understood Aaron's concern for the health of the animal. She also noticed immediately how the horse and girl seemed very attached. Jillian began rubbing the mare's forehead, and the horse responded by lowering her head to encourage the itching around her cheeks, eyes, and ears. Jillian had begun a steady stream of hushed words she murmured to the mare, and Jamila seemed to be listening. The scene took Allison a moment to absorb. She couldn't deny the look of love on her granddaughter's face. Jillian wore a serene smile she'd never seen before, and for a moment, she saw her daughter's expression in the face of her granddaughter. She could sense emotions hovering close to the barriers the girl normally carried. Allison felt the prick of tears. She had never seen her granddaughter so happy.

"Come pat her, Grandma. She is super nice, and don't worry, she won't bite." Jillian couldn't tell if her grandmother was scared of the horse or just worried about how skinny she was. It was weird that in just three weeks, she had become accustomed to seeing Jamila's bones poking out. She saw the beauty in the horse's eyes and heart rather than her physical body.

"Oh, my." Grandma Allison exhaled a long breath. "She is very thin. Poor thing," the old woman frowned. "Okay, dear, let's let her sniff my hand first. Isn't that what you are supposed to do? Like a dog sniffs your hand?"

"See, Grandma, she likes you.!" The mare gave Grandma Allison's hand a sniff and then lowered her head and poked out her muzzle so Grandma was forced to stroke her face.

Allison was surprised by how soft the mare's muzzle seemed. She continued to rub her forehead, and Jamila half-closed her eyes with appreciation. Once again, Allison was overcome with emotion. She was such a trusting kind being even after the neglect and starvation she'd suffered. Allison suddenly understood why Jillian felt a strong attraction to the sweet creature.

Jillian was watching her grandmother closely. She could tell Grandma was enjoying petting Jamila, and obviously, Jamila was happy too. She allowed herself a spark of hope that perhaps her grandmother would agree and allow her to keep the horse.

"She certainly is a sweet thing, isn't she?" Grandma Allison said. "Well, I'm not going to decide right now. I would like to speak to the rescue director first so I can learn the responsibilities of owning a horse. But it isn't a 'no.' Not right now."

Jillian squealed with delight, surprising Jamila who raised her head, and before Jillian could jump in front of her grandmother, Jamila let out a loud snort and covered her grandma in snot. Jillian's joy turned to horror as she saw the shocked look on Grandma Allison's face, but shock faded into a grim smile, then resolved into a grin as her grandmother said dryly, "I guess that means she agrees?" Turning to Jamila she said, "Next time just nod your head, okay, girl?" As if she understood, Jamila bobbed her head up and down.

Bill was watching the scene unfold, his thick arms crossed over his massive chest. The red-haired orphan girl and the thin young horse had brought nothing but happiness to his home. He enjoyed spending time with the mare just for the company, but even more, he liked watching the two of them interact and learn from each other. The odd pair added a welcome new focus to fill the empty space left by the loss of his wife. Seeing the spark in Jillian's eyes when she played with the horse brought light to his otherwise dull existence, and he was relieved her grandmother seemed willing to consider keeping the horse.

At the top of Bill's driveway—standing out of sight but within earshot—another man considered the scene. Aaron shook his head in frustration and anger. He couldn't believe it. His mother was going to let the kid keep that bag of bones. His resentment grew as he realized that getting his hands on his niece's money might not be as easy as it first seemed. He needed to find a way to ensure that $400 was the maximum Jillian ever got to spend on herself each month. The additional $1,600 from his sister's estate just covered what he earned in a month of odd jobs. It didn't matter that his sister left it to Jillian. If he didn't have to look for work all the time, it would be better for them all. Especially him. Aaron had started planning when his mother and Jillian headed to see the horse. Now, staring at the thick hedge of small, white flowers that fronted his mother's house, he had a flash of insight. He couldn't act today or maybe even tomorrow, but soon he'd take care of the problem, and he finally decided exactly how he was going to do it.

Jamila's Thoughts

*Feel my trust, Old One! Breathe my breath. No fear. Just love.
Play! Eat! Run! My Small One needs our love. Grass needs rain. Rain
needs sun. I feel your heart, Old One. You want peace. Love. My Small
One bears you inside. Guard her.*

*Your scent and The Small One's—my Heart—mingled. And
another: the Eater anger smell is faintly mixed. Beware black anger!
Guard Our Small One!*

CHAPTER 18 - Ride 'em, Cowboy!

"Jillian! Telephone" Grandma Allison called. "It's your friend Lila," she said, handing her granddaughter the phone.

"Hi, Jillian. My family is going to watch the bull riding and mutton busting at the Roadrunner tonight. Wanna come with us? It's pretty fun and loads of friends will be there. It's kind of the only thing to do on Saturday night around here anyway," Lila added.

"Um, sure. Hang on. I've gotta ask Grandma." Jillian turned to her grandmother who'd overheard the conversation. "Can I please?" She gave her best pleading look.

"Alright," said Grandma Allison. "Since you're so cute and pathetic," she joked.

"Yup, I can come. Is Aubrey coming?" Jillian asked

"I think so. My mom was talking to her mom earlier. I'm pretty sure her whole family is coming. We can pick you up on the way about 5:30 so we can have dinner first and find a seat. It gets crazy crowded if you wait too late to order dinner. It'll be fun."

"Okay, see you soon." Jillian hung up and spontaneously walked up to her grandmother and gave her a hug. "Thanks so much, Grandma. Do you want to go to?" It had just occurred to her that perhaps her grandmother would enjoy an evening out.

Surprised by the hug and even more by the invitation, Grandma Allison replied, "Thanks, sweetie. I'm too old to want to sit on a hard bleacher watching some young man try to pit his wits against a bull ten times his size. But I appreciate you asking"

The Stansons arrived at 5:30 to pick up Jillian, and the short ride to the restaurant was fun. The green SUV carried Lila, her parents, and her younger sister. Joanna was a contrast to her older sibling; they shared long glossy black hair and exotic looks, but while Lila had a sprinkle of freckles, she resembled her mother's Thai heritage. Joanna's eyes were wide and round like her dad's. The self-proclaimed almost fourth-grader was bent on telling jokes, but she kept forgetting the punch line and had to start over again and again. By the time they arrived at The Roadrunner, Jillian's sides ached from laughing so hard.

An icon of the New River area, the Roadrunner Bar & Grill had been hosting mutton busting and bull riding on Saturday nights for as long as most could remember. The sprawling restaurant, with its giant roadrunner sign, drew folks of all different backgrounds: families, bikers, cowboys and, occasionally, the Scottsdale elite. The fare, simple and hearty, could be taken to picnic tables in the large open yard or eaten on the deck by the bar or inside the restaurant. Country music blared as a live band courted the crowd, the notes mingling with the clink of glasses and laughter in the already packed outdoor dining area. It was loud and exciting.

The family lucked out when a group of bikers left a picnic table that stood under a tree festooned with white lights. They took their seats and Mr. Stanson went to get menus.

Jillian was wide-eyed at the array of people, the noise, and the upbeat atmosphere. She had to raise her voice to be heard. "What is mutton busting anyway? Do you like, beat up a sheep? What do you bust?".

"Ha, ha! You're funny. No, they don't beat up sheep," Lila giggled. "They try to ride them. I did it when I was younger. It's fun, but it can hurt if you land wrong. They help you get on, and you lie on top of the sheep and wrap your arms and legs around it and hold on for your life. Very sheepy smelling. I stunk like mutton for days! Jojo keeps saying she's going to try, but she keeps chickening out." Lila stuck her tongue out at her little sister.

"I could do it if I wanted," Joanna insisted. "But I'm dressed too nicely today," she pouted. Indeed, she was wearing a sleeveless flowered dress that looked adorable on her and was not suited for riding a sheep.

"Yeah, yeah, excuses, excuses. You're chicken!"

"Am not!"

"Are too!"

"Girls! Stop arguing," Mrs. Stanson interrupted.

Subdued, the sisters just gave each other dirty looks. Lila's dad came back with the menus, and they ordered as soon as they could find a waitress. Everyone wanted to get to the bleachers that rose behind a tall fence at the back of the yard. Jillian could smell horses and cattle. Their scents mingled with the tang of barbecue, french fries, fried chicken, and beans creating an atmosphere that made Jillian feel she'd arrived in the Wild West. There wasn't much conversation as they ate their meal; each was busy people watching and feeling a growing excitement.

Stuffed but eager to explore, Lila and Jillian got permission to go in search of Aubrey. "She said she'd be here by now, so maybe she missed us and is already sitting in the bleachers. Let's go take a look." Lila led the way through the wide yard, winding their way past picnic tables full of families. Children of all ages ran about laughing and yelling. At the back of the yard near the restaurant stood a stage, which hosted the country band. The girls stopped for a minute to watch the musicians play. Jillian couldn't remember the last time she had heard live music. Her mom loved to go to concerts, and they used to go to the St. Michelle Winery music festival each year. But they missed last year and now—

Jillian caught Lila's arm. "Let's keep looking!" she yelled over the loud music, and the two continued on through the gate to the arena and bleachers.

The oval-shaped arena was centered in a fenced, outdoor stadium. It had a dirt floor and lots of banners from different sponsors plastered the sides of the metal railings. On the far side were three cattle-holding pens and chutes that led from behind the far wall to the pens. The bleachers rose up in an arc around three sides and were already filling with spectators. Cowboys and other young folks hung off the rails and milled around the sides of the ring. The excitement was

Jillian scanned the seats to see if she could spot Aubrey and the rest of her family. "There. On the far side. See?" she pointed them out to Lila. They worked their way around the arena, dodging strollers and chatting moms. They were halfway there when Jillian saw a flash of brown curls on a cowboy leaning on the rail just in front of her. Lila also saw who it was and winked at Jillian before continuing on. Turning around, unaware that Jillian was behind him, Trace bumped straight into her knocking her forehead on his chin.

"Ouch! What the—" Trace looked up, startled. "Oh, whoa. I'm sorry, Jillian! Hey, are you okay?" he asked, rubbing his chin.

"I'm okay. I may have a slight concussion or perhaps a brain bleed, but I think I'll live," Jillian quipped, rubbing the top of her forehead. "Are you here with your family?" she asked.

"Just my dad. He's sitting over there." Trace pointed to the other side of the arena. "I'm going to be riding." He blushed all of a sudden feeling self-conscious.

"Ride? You mean mutton busting?"

"Ha! That's funny. No, not mutton busting—that's for little kids—I'm going to ride a steer."

"You mean a bull?"

Trace shook his head.

"What's the difference between a steer and a bull?" Jillian frowned, not understanding the lingo.

"A bull is a male bovine. You know, ready to breed. And a steer is a male that's, um, been castrated. You know, he can't breed anymore." They were both a little uncomfortable with the topic, but it wasn't too weird. "Steers don't buck as hard as bulls do, so they let us ride them if they get permission from our folks. My dad signed the forms already, so I'm heading to pick my steer." He nodded to the announcer booth next to the entrance.

"Good luck," Jillian replied, feeling suddenly shy. "Um, I'll root for you, cowboy." Trace grinned, tipped his hat like an old-time cowhand and headed to the announcer's booth. Jillian shook off the strange sensations that took over when Trace stood near her and headed up the bleachers to join Aubrey, Lila, and their families.

The entertainment began with mutton busting. The announcer shared the rules with the crowd, and the first pair scrambled across the ring; the small blonde boy couldn't have been much older than five. Dressed in a helmet, flannel shirt, and blue jeans, he clung to the big white sheep. As it hopped and raced across the arena, the boy began bouncing and sliding sideways. By the time they reached the end of the arena and the sheep turned, the boy had lost his grasp and fell to the dirt. The audience cheered and he stood wiping his hands on his pants and hustled out of the ring.

Jillian could understand Joanna's hesitation to go and bust muttons, and she asked Lila if she'd really done it.

"Yup, I did it. Once. But I made it further than that kid. I didn't want to be called a chicken," she added, poking out her tongue at her sister who sat on the bench behind the three girls.

"You shouldn't be so hard on your sister," Aubrey scolded Lila. "Maybe she is smart and has a strong sense of self-preservation. I personally wouldn't want to try."

"Well, maybe she is, or maybe she's just a chicken." Lila wasn't going to budge.

After four unsuccessful attempts at clinging to the back of a sheep for more than eight seconds, the fifth rider—a six-year-old girl dressed in a cute pink cowgirl outfit— managed to make it to the buzzer. The crowd cheered and the next event was announced.

"Ladies and gentleman, boys and girls!" the announcer called to quiet the crowd. "Our next event is steer riding. This contest is open to young men and women between the ages of eleven and fourteen. If your parents have signed all the paperwork and you're entered, come on down to the chutes. It's about time to begin. Just a reminder, no slapping or touching the steer with your hands. You must stay on for at least eight seconds. Our esteemed judges will give points. A total of fifty possible points for the rider, and fifty possible points for the steer. Now, let's hear it for all our hopefuls!" The crowd clapped and whistled as the kids lined up ready for the fun to begin.

Jillian spied Trace waiting for his turn to ride. She was nervous for him. The first rider barely made it out of the chute. The steer wasn't really bucking, but it spun to the right as it burst out of the gate unseating its rider within two seconds. Jillian thought the steer looked satisfied as it trotted to the back of the arena where the exit gate had opened.

The next two riders fared a little better than the first. The second steer left the gate slowly, looked around, and started forward. Its rider seemed unsure what to do at first, but he began spurring the steer, and it humped its back sending the unprepared rider to the ground.

The following rider, an older boy Jillian recognized from school, got bucked off in four seconds. Next up was Trace.

"Look who's coming up," Lila pointed to Trace, then clapped her hands. The three girls watched as he swung his leg over the bull standing on the rails just over it. He eased down, and slipped his right hand under the bucking strap, which encircled the steer's girth just behind its shoulder. The steer, a brown and white animal of medium size, lunged forward in the chute, and the cowboys who were helping Trace on the rail, grabbed him and held him steady. When Trace had tightened his rope and had a good grip, he nodded to the gatekeeper, and the chute flew open.

Unlike the last two animals, Trace's steer came out of the chute bucking. The crowd jumped to its feet cheering for him. Jillian held her breath, and Lila grabbed her hand and Aubrey's and squeezed tight. Jillian was amazed at how Trace managed to stay on top of the bucking beast. The clock was ticking, and at seven seconds, it looked like he was going to get thrown. The steer suddenly quit bucking and spun to the right coming to a stop before kicking its hind legs up in the air again.

Trace hung on, and finally, the buzzer sounded. He made it. He rode the steer for eight full seconds. He even managed to hop off and land on his feet. The three girls jumped up and down joining the crowd that chanted, "Eight seconds! Eight seconds!" Trace gave a gracious bow to the audience and strode out to greet his dad, who was whooping and hollering at the exit gate.

CHAPTER 19 - Eight Seconds

Jillian felt a combination of pride and relief. Trace had made it without getting hurt, and so far, was the only boy to ride to the buzzer. She wanted to go and congratulate him but then thought it was silly. She'd come to watch with her friends, and that's what she was going to do.

"Jason's up next. He's a grade up from us, and he goes on my bus. He lives pretty close to me on Circle Mountain. They say," Lila added, lowering her voice so that Aubrey and Jillian leaned close, "that his father was in prison and got out six months ago. I heard he isn't a very nice man, and I feel sorry for Jason. He is kind of a jerk though too. Anyway, last year he did really well in steer riding and won a bunch of buckles and some money. He's definitely Trace's toughest competition."

Jillian watched as the stocky teen climbed on top of the chute ready to seat himself on the steer. His dark hair was cropped close and his eyes were focused on the steer. He was bigger than Trace—heavier by at least fifteen pounds and taller by two inches. He slid down to sit on the steer, readying his rope, and pulling it tightly across his right hand so he had a firm grip. He nodded to the gatekeeper.

His steer, like Trace's, began bucking at once. The boy seemed almost too big for the steer, his legs practically reached the ground, but the animal was giving it everything he had. It spun to the right and bucked twice, and then spun to the left, knocking Jason from his center. An unexpected roar came from the boy as he clung to the steer holding on only with his legs as he began to slide down the right side of the bucking animal. One final jump away from unseating the falling cowboy and the buzzer rang. It was so close! Had he made it? The judges were talking.

Jason stood up slowly. He had been tossed pretty hard by the steer. The crowd was cheering, but you could tell he wasn't listening. He walked intently to the judges and climbed up the rail in front of them to learn if he had made the buzzer. Jillian could see him arguing with one of the judges until he dropped back into the arena, shaking his head, and stomping out.

"Well, folks, that was a mighty fine ride by Jason Entibarra, but the judges have conferred and agreed that he almost made that buzzer. Almost! 7.9 seconds. Can you believe it?" The crowd booed and then laughed. "Young Jason was our champ last year, and he's sure to be back. Let's hear it for a great ride!" The crowd cheered.

"It looks like folks that's the end of our steer riding tonight. We're gonna congratulate Trace Carter for making it the whole eight seconds! Head on into the ring son and get your buckle and your cash. A hundred bucks ain't nothing to sneeze at. Let's hear it for our winner, Trace Carter!"

Trace collected his winnings from center ring and left the arena with a quick wave and flush in his cheeks. The announcer went on to proclaim a twenty-minute break.

Aubrey and Lila wanted to show Jillian the bulls that the public were allowed to view from behind a stout fence at the back of the arena. Their parents agreed, so the trio went in search of the cattle pens.

Squeezing through the milling throng, they passed through a gate along the high fence that separated the cattle pens and the chutes. Jillian was awed by the size of the beasts. She had seen cattle before from the road and during family outings to the fair, but standing less than ten feet from the huge bulls that bucked in the semi-pro rodeo circuit made her feel tiny. One of the giants tossed his head toward them pawing the ground. His muscles bulging at his shoulders. Snot flew as he snorted at the girls.

"They're gigantic," Jillian exclaimed, mouth open at the size and majesty of the huge animals. "But their kinda gross. Yuck!" she added, eyeing the thread of goo that hung from the bull's nostril.

"I know. Cool, huh?" Aubrey smiled. "They truck them to different rodeo events. Some of the bulls that make it to the big leagues are worth millions."

"No way." Jillian couldn't believe it.

"Ya huh," Lila affirmed. "Maybe we should get into the bull business. You know, we could raise them and then sell them for big bucks! Now that's a 'bull-et' proof idea!"

"No, Lila, your idea is 'bull-loney,'" quipped Aubrey.

"We couldn't take care of those huge things, they'd 'bull-doze' us." Jillian joined the fun.

"Quit 'bull-ying me,' Lila giggled, and they laughed until she started snorting, making them laugh even harder.

As they worked to gain control of the giggles, Jillian saw the boy Jason and a man who must have been his dad at the back of the pens. His father was yelling at him, though with the band playing and speakers blaring, it was impossible to hear what he said. She could see him, red-faced, screaming at his son who stood, shoulders hunched, staring at the ground. Jillian turned to see if the others had noticed, but they were next to the pen. When she looked back, Jason was gone. His father saw her gaze, and he glared at her with furrowed brows. His son resembled him, dark haired and dark eyed, though far larger in stature than his dad. Mr. Entibarra walked down the aisle toward Jillian scowling at her as he passed. She was embarrassed and surprised to have witnessed the argument between father and son, but the anger with which he looked at her almost felt like a physical slap.

"Whoa," Lila exclaimed as she neared Jillian. "What did you do to tick him off? He looked at you with dagger-eyes!"

"I don't know. I saw him yelling at his kid, that boy Jason. I guess he saw me watching him. I feel sorry for Jason. I get the feeling his dad was mad because he didn't win."

"We need to get back to my parents. The bull riding is going to start soon," Aubrey interrupted, and the girls left the bulls and made their way back to their seats.

They arrived to see Mr. Carter talking with Aubrey's folks. Trace was with him wearing his new buckle.

"Congratulations, cowboy!" Jillian grinned at Trace and earned a smile in return. His green eyes sparkled with pride. "That was a great ride, or at least it seemed that way to me," she added.

"It was a great ride," piped Lila. "I don't know how you hung on 'til the buzzer. And I thought mutton busting was hard!" She couldn't resist a glance at Joanna, who ignored her.

"I gotta say that eight seconds seems like a really long time when the thing you're riding isn't happy about it." Trace laughed. "Since the steer earns half of the possible points, you always want to pick one that will buck well, but hopefully not too well," he grinned.

"Well, I was impressed," Jillian answered. She was feeling weird again, kind of fluttery and stupid. Just then, much to her relief, the announcer began to speak, and they all focused on the arena where the first bull was being readied.

Jillian was unprepared for the explosive bucking style of these bulls. Their huge leaps and kicks made the steers seem tame in comparison. When the first rider was at seven seconds, the bull leaped high in the air, all four feet off the ground, and twisted violently to the left dumping his rider hard in the dirt. The second, third, and fourth riders fared no better. Not one was able to make it to the buzzer. The fifth rider, a small, lean cowboy wearing a thick protective vest and safety helmet, had just gotten on his bull when it began thrashing in the chute. The surrounding cowboys grabbed the rider by his arms and struggled to pull him out of danger. The massive bull had the rider's leg pinned and was leaning on it with all his weight. The rider cried out, and finally the bull moved so he could be dragged back out of the chute. The audience was silent. All were transfixed watching the medics wheel the cowboy off on a stretcher. The bull was sent back to the pen without a ride.

Jillian worked to slow her pounding heart. She hadn't expected anyone to get hurt. Bull riding was a lot more dangerous than she realized.

"Is he going to be okay, Mommy?" Joanna asked her mom, her eyes huge with fear and concern.

"Yes, honey. He'll be okay. They're going fix his leg right up." Mrs. Stanson comforted her.

As the sixth rider was ready to mount, they all held their breath. Thankfully, it was a clean mount, and the bull burst through the gate bucking and spinning to the right. The rider held on tight, and to the delight of the crowd, stayed on for a full eight seconds. His successful ride broke the tension, and the audience cheered with gusto. The seventh and eighth riders also managed to stay on until the buzzer, and Jillian was relieved when the ninth cowboy also stuck his bull.

On the drive home, after inviting Jillian over the next day to visit, Lila asked, "So what do you think of bull riding?"

"I don't know," Jillian answered. "It is super exciting and the bulls are humongous, but it seems awfully dangerous. I don't know why those riders would risk their necks just to sit on a bull for eight seconds. I mean, it seems kind of silly. You know what I mean?"

"Yeah, I know. Boys aren't terribly smart though. I mean, truly."

Jillian thought of Trace riding the steer. It had seemed courageous of him - not terribly intelligent, but daring. "Yeah, I guess you're right," she replied. "Boys aren't terribly smart. Brave perhaps, but not always smart."

CHAPTER 20 - Friends, Food, and Mystery

Jillian was excited to visit Lila's house. Aubrey and her mom picked her up on the way there. Like Aubrey, Lila had a pool where they planned to hang out and swim. Lila had organized an elaborate brunch menu she'd been preparing all morning. The girls were looking forward to tasting her latest creations.

Circle Mountain Drive wasn't far down New River Road. Aubrey thought the name was dumb since the road only went part way around the big flat-topped mountain that stood by the main road, angled like a wedge. The homes were newer and sat on two to five-acre lots. Jillian saw many different types of horse housing along the road, from solid-sided barns to pole buildings and metal-framed mare motels. As they drove west, closer to the hills, the open desert hillside was dotted with cactus and scrub. It was beautiful in a wild way.

Lila's house was off the main road, and as they drove through the circular drive, Jillian could see Lila waving at them in the arched doorway of her Spanish-style home.

"Come inside and eat. I can't wait for you to taste what I made," Lila bubbled, beckoning them in. From the moment she entered, Jillian fell in love with Lila's house. The floor was made of square red stone tiles and the walls were stucco. The doorways arched to the high ceilings and big wooden ceiling fans moved the air. The Stanson home was filled with tropical colors in rich jewel tones. Paintings by Polynesian artists hung on the walls, interspersed with family photos, mostly of Lila and Joanna.

"I love your home," Jillian declared. "It's so colorful and cozy. Where do the paintings come from?"

"I have a grandma and grandpa who live in Hawaii, on Maui. We get to visit them every year. My dad grew up there, and we lived there when we were little. It's so gorgeous in Hana where they live. We got most of the artwork from Hawaii, but some are from Thailand where my mom's family lives."

"Whoa, that's cool to have a grandma in Hawaii. And Thailand. I wish mine lived in Hawaii, except I wouldn't have met you, so I guess maybe not." Jillian grinned at her friend. "Hey, where's your sister, Joanna? I thought she'd be here. She is so funny."

"She's at her friend's house for the day. I wanted you two all to myself, and she is a pain in the neck sometimes. I love her, but you know how little sisters can be. Cute but annoying."

Jillian wished she had a sister. She'd wavered back and forth when her parents were alive, wanting a sibling to play with yet enjoying being spoiled and having her parent's focus on her alone. How different things would be today if she had a sister—she wouldn't be alone. But she wasn't alone. Not right now anyway. She was with her friends about to have a fun day of eating and swimming.

"Well, where is all the food you promised? I'm starving," Aubrey said.

The girls arranged themselves around the granite kitchen counter that was spread with an array of bowls and platters. The food looked delicious and smelled even better. Neither Aubrey nor Jillian had eaten breakfast and both of their stomachs rumbled in reaction to the scrumptious scent.

"See, even my tummy is telling you to serve it up!" Aubrey laughed.

Lila proudly read her menu off a scrap of paper, while pointing to each dish. "Okay, first, we have tropical fruit salad with organic yogurt and secret spices. Next, I made scrambled eggs with fried tofu and cherry tomatoes and homemade parmesan chips—that are to die for. You gotta try them. Next, I made homemade banana-pineapple muffins with prickly pear cactus jelly. And to drink, we have a blend of orange, mango and pineapple juice."

"Holy wow," Aubrey exclaimed. "I'm ready now. That all sounds so yummy. Let's eat."

The food was so good and plentiful, it was a while before anyone spoke again.

Stuffed after their brunch and banned from swimming for an hour by Mrs. Stanson—despite protests that the notion was old fashioned nonsense—the girls decided to take a walk.

Setting off toward the end of Lila's road, they were chattering about their meal and their plans to see who could swim underwater the longest. Jillian knew she was no competition for her friends. They both had pools and had been swimming in them for most of their lives. Jillian knew how to swim but wasn't a natural in the water.

"I'm going to beat you," Lila grinned up at Aubrey, who was several inches taller than her dark-haired friend. "I'm part fish, or at least my dad says so. Been swimming in the ocean, body surfing since I was a little kid. You can try, Aubs, but I don't think you'll be able to catch me," she teased.

"Well, we shall see, short stuff. I'm on the swim team, remember?" Aubrey winked at Jillian, who laughed at the bickering between the two. "I think we need to figure out some kind of prize for the winner. How about the loser has to—"

Aubrey's proposal was cut short by the gut-wrenching sound of an animal scream. The girls looked at each other in surprise.

"Who lives down here?" Aubrey asked.

"We're almost to the end of the road. That's where Jason Entibarra lives," Lila answered with concern. "I've seen their stock trailer going back and forth for months. I heard that Jason's dad is doing some horse trading, but I'm not sure if it's true. They have a tall wooden fence that hides their place from the street, so I've never seen inside."

"Something's going on down there." Jillian's stomach was still clenched from the sound of the scream they'd heard. "I think we should take a look." She regarded her friends, eyebrows raised. Lila and Aubrey looked at each other.

"Are you going to get us into trouble again?" Aubrey asked. "'Cause the last time you went after something, it turned out to be a mountain lion, and I'm not really up for that kind of adventure."

"We won't get into trouble," Lila interjected. "We can just take a peek. The fence has some gaps. We won't go in, just look." She looked pleadingly at Aubrey. "C'mon, Aubs, don't be so sensible. Nothing's going to happen. We'll take a look and then walk home and eat choc—"

Another scream split the air. It was definitely a horse, and it was coming from behind the tall fence at the end of the road. In instant agreement, the three girls crept silently toward the fence. Lila took the lead and gestured to a spot in the wood that had split leaving just enough room to see inside. Lila peered through the crack, but then jerked back just as a third scream, coming from directly behind the fence, nearly burst their eardrums. It was followed by the growling voice of an angry man spitting out curses at the horse.

Jillian nudged Lila away and squinted through the crack. It was hard to get a good look at the whole scene, but what she saw caused her to jerk backward in shock and disgust. Aubrey took her turn, and they all wore the same horrified expression.

Aubrey beckoned for them to walk back up the road holding a shushing finger in front of her lips. They walked more than a block before saying a word. Lila was the first to speak.

"I can't believe what I saw. Was that horse still really alive? That poor thing." Tears leaked from her eyes and Jillian felt hers moisten in response.

"We need to call Jennifer, right now." Jillian knew Jennifer would be able to help. What they'd seen was so awful she couldn't believe someone could do that to an animal.

"Who's that?" Lila asked

"She is the Director of Healing Horses, the rescue in Desert Hills," Aubrey answered for Jillian. "Let's go!" They ran the rest of the way to Lila's house.

"You gotta come right now," Jillian pleaded the moment Jennifer answered the phone. "He's gonna kill that poor horse, Jennifer. I swear, it's almost dead. Please come!"

Jennifer could tell from the pitch of her voice that Jillian was terrified. She calmly answered, "Hold on now, sweetie. First, you need to tell me where you are. Then, you need to explain exactly what happened and what you saw. I'll get in my truck while we're talking and come to you right away. What is your address?"

Jillian handed the phone to Lila, and Lila provided the address to Jennifer, and then gave the phone back to Jillian. "Okay, are you on the way?"

"Yes. I only live a few miles down the road, near Cave Creek. I'll be there in fifteen minutes. Now, please, try to tell me what you saw."

"Well, me and Lila and Aubrey were walking down Lila's road, and we were almost at the end when we heard a really awful scream. It sounded like an animal that was hurt. We were deciding whether we should peek through the fence when it happened again, but this time we could tell it was a horse for sure. Oh, Jennifer, it was just horrible! We looked through the fence and that man, Mr. Entibarra, had this poor horse all tied up like a hog. All its legs were lashed together, and he was beating it with a chain. It was terrible. The poor horse was trying to struggle, and it was screaming and screaming. Please hurry, Jennifer. I really think he could kill the poor thing. It is all skin and bones, like Jamilla when we found her, only maybe worse. Please hurry!"

"It sounds like we'll need to call the sheriff. I'm going to hang up and do that, and I will meet you at your friend's house. Stay where you are. Don't go back." Jennifer disconnected and Jillian hung up the phone. Mrs. Stanson was listening to her side of the conversation, and Lila filled her in on the details.

"You girls stay inside, please. You wait for the lady to come, okay? I don't want you in trouble or anyone getting hurt," Mrs. Stanson commanded with her Thai accent, her concern for the girls etched on her face.

"It's okay, Mama," Lila reassured her. "We'll stay inside. Let's go to my room while we wait," she said to Aubrey and Jillian.

If she hadn't been so shell-shocked by what they'd seen, Jillian would have instantly noticed that Lila's room was much like its occupant: chaotic, fun, and filled with hand-made art, cookbooks, and family photos. Her full-sized bed was piled with comfy pillows in bright greens and blues that matched the colors in her tropical-print quilt. A wicker nightstand held a lamp with a shade made of seashells that cast crazy shadows on the walls. An open cookbook lay on the quilt and several others were stacked on her matching wicker dresser. The lighting in the room was muted by a hand-painted silky cloth she had hung from the ceiling. It draped under the light and gave the feeling you were inside of a tent.

Despite the fear that had almost choked her, Jillian let the vibrant colors and upbeat photos help her relax. It was hard to believe just a few minutes ago they'd viewed the most awful thing they had seen in their young lives, and now here they were in a magical room that seemed to deny the existence of wickedness.

"What a pretty room."

"Thanks." Lila shone with pride. She told them of the hours she spent decorating and redecorating her room each month. The artwork and photographs—mostly hers—were periodically taken down and stored, and then re-hung when she was in the mood. Her latest display of photos depicted a row of poppy seed muffins photographed up close from a variety of angles. They were really quite clever, Jillian thought.

Aubrey flopped on the bed, tummy down, her long arms folded under her chin. "I can't believe what we just saw, you know? I still feel sick. How can anyone do that to a poor horse? I mean, guys, did you see how skinny it is? I can't believe it's still alive. I heard Jason's dad was in prison for years and got out six months ago, right, Lila?"

"That's what I heard," Lila replied. "I don't know why he was in jail. Stealing, I think? I'm not sure. Oh my gosh, Jason must know what's going on."

"Well, we don't know anything more than what we saw," Aubrey answered. "But a horse doesn't get that skinny overnight." She frowned, furious and disgusted at the thought.

"Don't you think he would have seen the horse? I don't know how he could just watch an animal in so much pain. I wonder if there are any more horses like that? They have a pretty big property, but the fence really hides it. I've seen their trailer go back and forth at least a few times a week. I sure hope, if there are other horses there, they're okay."

"You said he does horse trading. What does that mean? Do you just swap horses or something like that?" Jillian felt kind of silly not understanding.

"I don't know why they call it 'trading,'" answered Lila, "when it's really selling. A horse trader finds cheap horses and sells them for more money. Sometimes they find sick or skinny horses, then feed and resell them. Sometimes they get unbroke horses or wilder horses who are hard to handle, and they work with them 'til they can be ridden—then they sell them. Sometimes they get free horses who are too wild or hurt to resell to the public, and they send them to the kill buyers for cheap. It's all about making money. I know there are some nice people around here that do it who aren't abusing the horses or starving them. What we saw was awful!"

Jillian couldn't get the image out of her head. She didn't know what was worse: the man's face so full of rage and fury or the look of terror in the horse's eyes as it struggled to avoid the blows and free itself.

CHAPTER 21 - Investigations

Jennifer arrived, as promised, just fifteen minutes after their call. Her white truck with the Healing Horses logo on the side was followed by a county sheriff's car. They reached the front door of Lila's house together. Jillian introduced Jennifer to Mrs. Stanson and Lila. Jennifer remembered Aubrey from their adventures the week before.

"This is Sheriff Sorenson," Jennifer introduced the tall, uniformed man beside her. He tipped his hat to Mrs. Stanson and shook her hand. His white hair was neatly trimmed, his blue eyes friendly.

Turning to the girls, the sheriff pulled a little spiral pad out of his shirt pocket. "Hi, girls. Jennifer told me you saw something pretty terrible. I know it's not easy to talk about, but can you please tell me exactly what you heard and saw? I'm going to take some notes." The girls nodded.

"Let's start with what time this happened," the sheriff began.

Lila responded, "It was right after we ate, so around eleven-thirty. We were full and decided to take a walk before we went swimming. We were just talking when we heard a terrible scream. It was loud and came from down the road. We weren't sure what it was at first. It spooked us. We were deciding whether to go see what it was when something screamed again. This time we could tell the cry came from a horse." Lila shuddered at the memory of the dreadful sound.

Jillian took over. "We had to do something, so we went to the fence and found a crack that we could see through. It was so scary and the horse was bleeding! The man, Mr. Entibarra, had tied the poor thing's legs together and he was yelling at the horse and hitting it with a chain. The poor horse kept screaming. I don't know if it's still alive Sheriff," she said, her eyes glistening with emotion. She couldn't get the terrible picture out of her mind.

The sheriff stood up and looked at Jennifer. "I'm glad you girls called Jennifer. And I'm especially glad you didn't go onto the property or intervene. We don't want you getting hurt, and it's easier to prosecute a case if there has been no outside interference. I'm going to call in my deputy, and when he gets here, we'll go take a look." With that, he walked back to his car to call on his radio.

"What are they going to do?" Lila asked the obvious question.

Jennifer explained, "In this type of case because you said there was violence and the horse was tied and bleeding, it warrants the sheriff to investigate. He will go to the property and ask Mr. Entibarra if he will show him the horse voluntarily. If the property owner isn't agreeable, then the sheriff will have to get a warrant to be able to get in and examine the animals and property.

"If the animals are in physical danger—and it sounds like that in this case— then we will assess the health of each horse and determine if and when it can be moved. We work very closely with the Sheriff's office." Turning to Jillian, she said, "I'm really glad that you called me. If you ever happen across another bad situation like this and you can't reach me, please call 911, and they will connect you with the Sheriff. You girls did just the right thing."

Within minutes the deputy arrived. Younger than the sheriff by twenty years, with a boyish face, hazel eyes and a quick smile, Deputy Clarke greeted the girls and tipped his hat to Jennifer and Mrs. Stanson.

The sheriff and his deputy walked to the edge of the road and began to plan their approach. The property was three blocks away and was surrounded by an eight-foot-tall wood fence on at least the two sides that were visible from the road. A butte rose up along the far side of the ranch making entry or escape in that direction impossible. The entry and exit gates were the only access to the property. They concluded their plan, and the sheriff explained to Jennifer, "We're going to drive down a couple blocks and park our cars across the road to create a roadblock. You stay well behind the trucks, please, until we've gained access. I'll call you on your cell, okay?"

"Okay, Sheriff. Let me know if we need more than one trailer. I can have ours here in fifteen minutes, but it will take another hour to gather up any more if you want them." The sheriff nodded and got into his truck and drove off. Turning to the girls, she said, "Don't even ask. You need to stay at least two blocks away, or better yet, go back inside." Her brow furrowed. "Stay out of the way, okay?" Jennifer looked pointedly at Jillian and strode off down the street.

"Do we really have to go inside?" Lila looked at Aubrey and Jillian. "We don't have to get in the way, but I know a place where we can hide, and I think we'll be able to see what happens."

"Didn't you just hear what the rescue lady said?" Aubrey frowned at Lila. "We should go back inside and wait 'til everything is over and they say it's safe."

"It will be perfectly safe, Aubs. C'mon! We'll stay hidden and no one will know. Aren't you even the slightest bit curious? What if something exciting happens and we miss it. Nothing exciting ever happens to me." She pouted.

"What Jennifer said was, 'stay out of the way, at least two blocks away.' Is the hiding place two blocks away, Lila?"

Jillian asked, again siding with Lila. "You don't have to come, Aubrey, if you really don't want to. I just want to see what happens to the poor horse."

"I know. I saw the horse," Aubrey relented, a sad look on her face. "I don't like breaking the rules, you guys know that. But I guess if we stay hidden and out of the way…"

"Cool! Okay, follow me."

Lila led the way across the street and down the other side of the road. Two blocks away, a dirt road turned left up a small incline. On the corner lot, a slanted pile of weathered wood and glass was all that was left of a house. A little past the rubble stood a sand-blasted metal shed; crumpled at one end, it offered a clear view of the front of the Entibarra ranch yet provided good cover.

The girls walked up the dirt road to the driveway of the abandoned home, then tiptoed to the shed where they hunkered down to wait.

The two county sheriff trucks sat facing each other across the road just before the ranch. The deputy stood at the very end of the road, in front of the far gate near the butte. The sheriff was halfway down the block walking toward the entry gate, and Jillian could see Jennifer standing on the sidewalk beyond the two trucks. Lila was right—the view was perfect.

Sheriff Sorenson paused at the same crack in the wood that the girls had found. He bent down to peer through the fence. Unlike the girls, he didn't flinch but spent what seemed like a long time studying the scene beyond the barrier. When he stood back, anger clouded his expression and he clenched his fists and drew his handgun. The three girls looked at each other with surprise.

The sheriff approached the automatic gate and pushed the buzzer on the keypad. He leaned toward the speaker mounted above the keypad. "Mr. Entibarra, this is Sheriff Sorenson of Maricopa County. I'd like to speak with you. Please open the gate." He straightened up and waited. One minute, two minutes, after three minutes, he pushed the intercom again, speaking loudly, "Mr. Entibarra, I know you're there. Let me come in and talk. We just have a few questions. I need you to open the gate."

Again, silence. The sheriff looked at his deputy who shrugged. Jillian could hear anger creep into his raised voice, "Mr. Entibarra. Please don't make me get a warrant. If you open the gate, we can talk here. But if you make me go and bother a judge for a warrant, I'm going to haul you down to the station. Now, just open the gate and we can talk."

All of a sudden, Deputy Clarke motioned to the sheriff he could hear a noise on the other side of the back gate. Then, as the gate creaked open, a small battered black truck burst through the widening gap, blasting through the gate, and heading straight for the deputy. Jillian's hand flew to her mouth to muffle her gasp of shock. The truck didn't slow down at all nor did it try to avoid hitting the man who stood ten feet away. The engine whined as Mr. Entibarra slammed on the gas and headed for the young cop.

The deputy leapt as quickly as he could to avoid the truck, but it clipped him on the right thigh as he dove out of the way, sending him flying through the air. He landed hard on the dirt road and lay unmoving.

Sheriff Sorenson, gun in hand, crouched in a firing position facing the oncoming truck. Aubrey covered her eyes. Jillian wanted to do the same, but she couldn't help but watch the truck bearing down on the sheriff. He had to do something!

Then, she saw him draw in a breath and aim his gun at the truck. He fired his gun three times, hitting the truck's right front tire twice and exploding the front right headlight. A loud "bang" sounded as the tire blew and the truck spun to the right, its forward motion causing it to flip over and roll twice before landing on its roof. When the dust settled, Jillian could see Mr. Entibarra pinned behind the wheel, his head bleeding.

Sheriff Sorenson approached the truck, gun drawn. He tried to open the driver's door, but it refused to budge. The roof had crumpled, trapping both doors closed. The only way out was to cut off the door. Sheriff Sorenson got on his radio and called for help.

Recovering from her shock, Jennifer ran straight to the deputy. He was barely conscious but said it was only his leg that hurt. Jennifer cautioned him to stay still as she crouched beside him examining his leg. The sheriff, worry contorting his expression, knelt down and let out a big breath. "Glad you're gonna be okay, buddy. I've got help on the way. Take it easy and stay put."

The girls looked at each other wide-eyed. Everything had happened so fast. "We'd better get out of here," Aubrey cautioned, and this time no one argued.

They scooted across the yard and down the dirt road to the main street and waited behind the two trucks. By this time, the few neighbors who were home were standing in their driveways, curious to know what was going on. Lila gave them the scoop.

Moments later, blaring sirens filled the air, as the fire department arrived. Two ambulances also pulled up, and three more sheriff cars screeched to a stop behind the trucks that blocked the road. In no time, paramedics were getting the deputy onto a stretcher, and Jennifer was standing to the side, arms crossed, a sick expression on her face. The girls watched as Sheriff Sorenson and two of the new officers entered the broken gate and disappeared behind the fence.

Meanwhile, a throng of firefighters cut open the door to the truck and extracted Mr. Entibarra who seemed confused. They heard "concussion" and "lucky to be alive" and the enormity of what happened finally sunk in. Jillian saw the glitter in Aubrey's eyes and felt her own tears as well. They held hands and waited for Sheriff Sorenson to reappear.

It seemed like hours before the sheriff and one of the other two men emerged. Jillian saw him walk straight to Jennifer and start to speak. She couldn't hear what was said, but it wasn't hard to get his meaning. Jillian felt her heart sink as he shook his head. It couldn't be good. They saw Jennifer pull out her cell phone and start making calls. The sheriff and his deputy walked back inside the compound and triggered the front electronic gate to open.

The three friends, holding hands, watched as Jennifer walked in the gate. Jillian was torn. She wanted to go and see what was happening on the ranch, but she was scared the horse might be dead, and she wasn't ready to see that. So they waited, eventually sitting on the side of the road, wondering what was occurring behind the barrier. The Healing Horses trailer arrived. Then another trailer and another. The drivers stood talking in a tight group outside the gates of the ranch.

The sun, well past its zenith, glared down. Jillian's light complexion was unused to the scorch of the sun's rays. She could feel the skin on her face tightening. She knew she was getting sunburned. The wait seemed impossibly long before Jennifer finally emerged, leading a horse the girls' hadn't seen before. Its hooves were so long that the poor horse looked like it had duck feet. Its ribs all showed, and Jillian thought it was a little thinner than Jamila was when she first found her.

They saw Jennifer talk to the group, then turn and head toward them, the same grim look on her face they had seen when she first entered the ranch. "Hey, girls. I wanted to let you know what's going on: there are eight horses on the property. None of them are in good condition, I'm afraid." She frowned. "The horse you saw is alive right now. He is untied but still down. I've got a veterinarian on the way to give us his advice. He has some pretty bad injuries, so we'll have to see.

"And you," she looked at the girls, "each of you get to take credit for saving them. It is very likely that at least one or two of the horses in there would have died within a day or two if you hadn't called.

"I know you are probably curious, but you can't go on the property and see the horses. The sheriff needs to do a lot of documenting and taking photographs. The horses will be taken to a Maricopa County facility to be evaluated, then they will likely be placed in our care. It's going to take a while, so you might as well go back home."

"But what about Jason? And his mom? Where are they? Did they know about this, I mean, how could they not?" Lila accused.

"Sheriff Sorenson learned that Jason and his mother left for Tempe to visit family this morning. I'm sure they will be contacted. Now go home and try to relax. We'll take care of these horses from here."

She turned to walk back to the ranch but stopped after two paces. Turning to Jillian, she offered, "Oh, and I got a call from your grandmother. She wants to visit the rescue with you and talk to me about Jamila. Please let her know that tomorrow will work just fine. I'll see you then."

Jillian thanked her but wondered how they'd get to the rescue. She'd be surprised if Aaron would give them a ride. Lila interrupted her thoughts. "Let's go back to my house. This is too sad."

CHAPTER 22 - Questions Answered

Mrs. McKinstry dropped Jillian at her grandma's an hour later, but instead of going inside, she walked next door to Bill's house to see Jamila. The thin Arabian mare nickered at her, tossing her blonde forelock as if to say, "Hurry up and scratch me!" Jillian smiled and felt her heart swell with gratitude. When they first met, this little horse was so much more like the ones she'd seen today. Now Jamila was gaining weight and revealing more of her personality as each day passed. Her coat was glossier and her eyes were full of curiosity. She was a long way from being fit and healthy, but the results of good care, love, and proper nutrition were beginning to show.

Facing Jamila, Jillian scratched both sides of her neck in the spot she knew the mare liked. Jamila responded by twitching her muzzle back and forth.

"You silly girl," Jillian murmured. "I'm so glad I found you. I don't know what I'd do if you weren't here. I can talk to you about anything, and you don't care what it is I say, do you? I felt so sad today, girl. I don't know why anyone would hurt a horse or any animal. Why would he do that?" she asked the mare, looking into her liquid brown eyes. "Why do people abandon horses? Or people? Oh, Jamila," Jillian began to weep, "why did my mom and dad have to die?"

Jillian reached her arms around Jamila's neck, and the mare lowered her head and bent her neck to return the hug. Jillian drew in the mare's comforting scent and let the tears fall until she felt her sadness fade. They stood like that for a long moment, each finding solace in the other.

Bill watched the tender interaction between Jillian and Jamila from his living room window. He knew Jillian still had a lot of emotions to process after the sudden death of her folks. It seemed that Jamila knew somehow too. *Animals are so intuitive.*

The next morning, Jillian asked Grandma Allison when they were going to Healing Horses to talk to Jennifer. "How are we going to get there, Grandma?" she asked.

"Don't worry about our ride. I have it figured out, and no, your uncle won't be joining us. We're going to leave here around 10:30."

"Can I please go and visit Jamila, Grandma? I get to lead her out of the corral today. Carefully, of course, 'cause she isn't super strong, but she's doing really great." Jillian's passion bubbled over and her grandmother couldn't help but smile and agree.

Allison felt grateful to the abandoned horse for helping Jillian adjust to life in Arizona. She knew it was a huge change for her young granddaughter. Arizona was so different from Washington State. The poor girl hadn't talked about her parents much at all since she arrived. Allison knew Jillian needed something to focus on, and the horse seemed to help. While Allison had never had any pets, she knew it gave the girl pleasure. There wasn't enough of that in Jillian's life right now.

Interested to learn how the adoption process at Healing Horses worked, Allison had many questions about the costs of keeping a horse. Would the $400 Jillian had to spend each month cover all the expenses? Of course, the entire $2,000 per month was Jillian's inheritance, not hers regardless of what Aaron said. Since her daughter and son-in-law had provided for her in their will by paying off her home mortgage, she now had more money to spend than she had for most of her life—at least as long as Aaron was contributing.

She frowned at the thought. She knew Aaron was opposed to spending any money on a horse. She may be old, but she wasn't stupid. Her son was lazy. It was disappointing to admit, but she'd known for years he had no ambition. He was twenty-nine years old and didn't have steady work. He lived at home and still acted like a sullen teenager. She figured he saw Jillian's inheritance as a windfall for himself and any minor efforts he'd been making to look for work were likely to end.

Perhaps I should have married again and provided Aaron a father figure. She sighed. She just couldn't bring herself to let go of her Sam. He'd died years ago, but it felt like it was only yesterday that cancer stole her husband. Her heart was still too full of love for Sam to think about marrying again. She had been lucky enough to find a true, deep love once in her life, and she knew how rare that was. So she wrapped herself in Sam's memory keeping him close to her heart.

Jillian was grooming Jamila when Bill came outside. "Hi, Jillian. Are ya ready ta lead 'er round a bit today?"

"You bet Bill." Jillian was happy to do something new with Jamila. She'd led the mare around the paddock, but they hadn't been out of the corral together since the day she arrived two weeks ago.

"How 'bout if ya put 'er halter on an' we'll give 'er a taste of some sweet green grass?" Bill patted Jamila on the neck and she snorted her agreement.

Jillian slipped her halter on and clicked on the lead rope. She held the loop in her left hand and took hold of the lead line in her right hand, about ten inches below Jamila's jaw. "Is this right?" she asked, looking up at Bill—confident that it was, but wanting assurance.

"Yep. Looks good, young lady. Now remember that it's likely she was never off Hank's place 'til now. Before we let 'er graze, why dontcha lead 'er up the driveway an' back a couple times. Hold the line tight, but remember what I told ya?" He paused waiting for her to answer.

"I remember. If she gets super scared and pulls really hard, then rather than getting dragged around, it's better to let her go. Oh, and don't get my hand caught in the loop of the rope." Jillian recited what she'd been taught. She didn't want to think about Jamila getting spooked and running away. She hoped that the mare wasn't going to test her strength. "You're gonna be a super good girl, right, Jamila?"

Bill opened the corral gate and Jillian led Jamila from the pen. They walked slowly up to the end of the driveway; the horse walked at Jillian's shoulder as if it were no big deal. When they reached the end of the drive, Jamila stopped and looked up the street toward her old home. For a moment she paused, nostrils flared, breathing in the scents around her. Then she turned toward Jillian looking at her questioningly as if to ask, "Okay, friend, what's next?"

They turned around and started back down the driveway. When they got to the bottom, she praised Jamila for being so calm. Three times the mare confidently walked up and back. Then Jillian led Jamila onto Bill's lush green lawn and the mare fell to grazing. The rip-tear-grinding sounds gave Jillian a peaceful feeling.

Jamila's Thoughts

Oh, joy, Small One! Touch makes happy. You lead, I follow. Always. Wait. I smell...scents of past: old herd makes sorrow. New herd makes joy!

Hairy-faced two-legger watches. Protects. Eater-safe. He has eaten his grey-green haze: swallowed the sorrow. Still, I see his loneliness leaking.

Less now. The Small One makes it leave. She makes all sorrow leave.
Only joy. Play. Touch. Follow. Life!

Bill sat on his front patio drinking a second cup of coffee, enjoying watching the little red mare and her red-headed human relaxing in the sun. For those few minutes, all three were at complete peace.

Jillian leaned on Jamila, listening to the rhythmic sound of her grazing and not thinking of anything at all. The mare was greedily munching the rich grass, enjoying every bite. The young girl smiled grateful for small favors and the sight and sounds of contentment.

When Jillian had put Jamila away, leaving her with a big kiss on her soft muzzle, she told Bill she was going with her grandma to visit Healing Horses and talk with Jennifer about Jamila.

"I know all about the visit. How'd ya think yer gettin' there?" Bill asked with a sly smile.

"Really?" Jillian exclaimed.

"Yup. I tole yer grandma that I'd be happy ta give ya a ride. I'd like ta see the place myself. Hop in my truck an let's go kiddo."

The ride to Healing Horses was oddly comforting. Jillian sat between the massive bulk of her neighbor and the lithe frame of her grandma. It felt good to be sandwiched between two people who cared about her. The ride took only fifteen minutes. Jillian felt hopeful about the outcome of the visit. Her fervent wish was that Grandma Allison would decide that she could keep Jamila. The day had started perfectly and, fingers crossed, it was going to get even better.

A pretty painted "Healing Horses" sign hung between two tall wooden poles welcoming visitors to the sanctuary. The dirt driveway led the way to the main building with pastures and turnouts on both sides. Jillian was surprised at the number of horses. They were all different sizes and colors grazing in the irrigated pastures or resting under shade covers in their turnouts. It looked like horsey heaven to Jillian.

The driveway led to a parking lot next to the main barn. Jennifer waved from the barn as she walked out to greet them. She wore her light brown hair tied back in a ponytail, a Healing Horse t-shirt, and a pair of faded jeans. Jillian admired the way she always looked so put together even in her simple outfit. Her mom had been the same way. Even when she first woke up with tousled hair and wrinkled nightgown, Mom somehow looked polished. Jillian couldn't tame her crazy curls, much less look organized or poised without a ton of effort, and even then, the results were sketchy.

"Hi, guys! I'm so glad you could make it," Jennifer welcomed them. Jillian introduced her grandmother, who shook Jennifer's slender hand.

"I'm so very glad to meet you, Jennifer. Jillian has told me much about you. And God bless you for helping all the animals. Heavens, it must be a lot of work."

Jennifer smiled in return. "It is a lot of work, and thank goodness for volunteers and for my farm manager Lisle. I know you have questions about Jamila. Let's chat in the conference room and then perhaps take a tour of the rescue if you like. Thanks for bringing them, Bill." She shook Bill's hand. "Shall we go?"

Grandma Allison nodded. "That would be lovely, dear."

"Great. Let's get started." Jennifer spoke to Jillian as they headed toward the office, a small single level building next to the barn. "Oh, and we'll be sure to visit the other horses in the group that came from Hank's place. We've kept them together, and they're steadily improving."

"That would be great. I'd love to see them." Jillian hoped they were improving as quickly as Jamila.

The front office was neat and homey. One wall held a board filled with thank-you notes from adopters and volunteers. There was a pretty wood computer desk in the front of the room and pictures of horses crowded the walls. They passed the empty desk and through a doorway to a medium-sized conference room. A long wood table was surrounded by comfortable swiveling chairs. The sideboard held an urn of hot water and an assortment of teas and a tray of cookies. Everyone took a seat.

Jennifer began, "I'm so glad you're here to learn about our adoption process and ask questions." She smiled at Grandma Allison, and continued, "Our process is straightforward and simple. We have an application and a questionnaire we will ask you to fill out. It's on our website, but I printed one out for you. Since you have been taking care of Jamila," she nodded at Bill and Jillian, "you know about her needs. We also do a site visit, but that's already been done. There is an adoption fee, but I spoke to the president of our Board of Directors, and she has agreed with me to reduce the fee by half. It will be $200 for you to adopt Jamila."

Jillian could barely contain herself. Could she really be adopting Jamila soon?

"I'll be scheduling our veterinarian, Dr. Longton, to come and check on Jamila. He'll evaluate her needs and give her some vaccines, and he will probably schedule a time to do some dental work. Oh, and the farrier should be contacting you to set a time to trim her feet."

"Oh, dental work?" Grandma Allison said. "What kind of dental work do horses need? Is it expensive?"

"Well not to worry, Mrs. Parker. We like to take care of any dental work before horses are adopted. But horses do need to have their mouth examined by a veterinarian each year to ensure there are no high points or problems in the teeth. It's much like getting your own teeth cleaned—it's good to get them checked out to avoid big problems. It costs about $125 for her teeth to be floated—that's what they call it when they grind their teeth.

"Some horses have wolf teeth, a bit like ours. Some don't. If they do, we normally extract them. It keeps the horse comfortable when wearing a bridle and bit."

"Okay, thank you, Jennifer. One time per year, is that right?"

"That's right. If you adopt Jamila, please plan on veterinary expenses. Horses need vaccines twice per year. We suggest you budget $600 to $900 per year for preventative care. That amount includes dental care. We've created a list of expenses and other information for potential adopters." She passed a white folder with the Healing Horse logo on the front to Grandma Allison. "We want to be sure people that are new to horse ownership know what kind of a commitment they are making. Most of the horses we rescue have experienced some kind of abuse or neglect. They deserve forever homes. Owning a horse is a long-term commitment," she looked at Jillian. "It means that even when you are in college, you will keep and care for Jamila."

Jillian nodded solemnly realizing for the first time that she was making a gigantic promise. It was a decision she would live with for a long time. Oddly, it wasn't scary.

"How long do horses live?" Grandma Allison asked.

"Horses can live up to forty years, but most live to their mid-twenties," Jennifer answered. Directing her comments to Jillian, she continued, "That means you could have Jamila in your life until you're forty-seven years old, Jillian. I want you to really think about what this means."

Turning back to Grandma Allison, Jennifer asked, "I have to ask this question. Um, can you please let me know how you intend to pay for Jamila's care? It's important for us to know you have the resources you'll need to properly take care of her."

To Jennifer's surprise, it was Jillian who responded. "I have my own money, Jennifer. My parents left me a monthly income and I get to spend $400 of it on myself or whatever I want. Will it cost more than $400 a month?" she asked, not having seen the papers in the folder Grandma Allison had in front of her. "I mean, if I have to spend more, I can, but I want Grandma to have the rest of the money to help us live."

Jennifer was impressed by Jillian's maturity. For a young girl who had recently lost her family, Jillian was unusually selfless. "I think that $400 per month will be more than enough to take care of Jamila. Here is the budget we suggest: $200 per month for feed and $50 for bedding. Our farrier charges $35 to trim feet, and $85 to shoe a horse every five to six weeks. Worming every six to eight weeks is another $12. In total, we recommend that our clients retain about $4,000 per year, per horse; although, you never can tell if you'll need emergency funds. It sounds like you'll have the expenses covered. Will Jamila be staying with Bill or moving to your house?"

Bill hadn't said a word since they arrived. Jennifer noticed him studying Jillian during the conversation, as if looking for doubt or discouragement.

"She kin stay with me 'til Jillian wants or needs ta move 'er. I'm purty attached ta that lil' mare too." He glanced at Jillian and she beamed back at him.

"Excellent. We have training classes for new horse owners. They must attend two short classes. I'm sure Jillian knows most of what we teach already, but it will be a good idea for her to sign up for the next classes, which start on Wednesday. Is there anything else you would like to know?"

Grandma Allison spoke up. "I think you have answered my questions. We will review the application, and I'll discuss this more with my granddaughter. To be honest, I've never considered owning a horse myself, so it is a bit overwhelming. However, if Bill is willing to let her stay with him for now," she paused. "Well, we'll talk about it. Thank you for taking the time to explain your process."

"Very good," exclaimed Jennifer, and she winked at Jillian. "Let's take a tour, shall we?"

CHAPTER 23 - The Good, The Bad, and The Ugly

Jillian was ecstatic. The meeting with Jennifer had gone better than she hoped. Her heart felt as if it would burst with excitement and anticipation. She was one step closer to adopting Jamila. She surprised her grandmother by taking her hand as they walked out of the office to view the Healing Horses facility.

Jennifer began their tour in the main barn. The center aisle was paved and there were giant fans set up at each end of the barn keeping air circulating for the horses. Jennifer explained their cooling system. "We keep the fans going during the day, and sometimes at night too. You'll notice the misters come on soon. Our system is set up to go off every two minutes during hot weather, and the stalls are all misted to keep the horses cool."

"Should I get Jamila a fan? Does she need a mister too?" Jillian asked.

"I think a fan is a great idea. You don't need to get the huge ones like we have here. There are several things you can do to help keep your horse cool. You'll learn about them in class next week."

"The horses we keep in the barn either require treatment, or they're not part of a social group. They have individual turnouts attached to each stall." They approached a big older looking horse in the first stall on the right. His dark brown coat almost matched his black mane and tail. His age was evident: grey patches showed under his eyes and on his cheekbones, his back was swayed.

"This is Jasper. He's had a rough life, I'm afraid. He came to us a year ago from a neglect situation. He was kept in a dog run for the last five years. His owners had no idea how to care for a horse. Considering how poor his living conditions were, it is amazing he still has love for people."

"Why do people treat horses like that, Jennifer? I don't understand."

"It's different in every case. The family that had this horse didn't know anything about him or about horses. They thought it would be fun for their kids to be able to ride around the neighborhood. Then the kids lost interest, and he was ignored and left in his pen. It's sad when people don't educate themselves about horse care and the commitment needed. Getting a horse in your family is exciting, as I'm sure you know Jillian, but you'd be surprised how many people don't have any idea of the responsibility."

"This guy," Jennifer turned to stroke Jasper's face, "is twenty-eight years old, and he's going to stay with us for the rest of his life. Right, buddy?"

"They certainly are lucky to have a place to live out their lives," commented Allison, eyeing the senior gelding.

"We're lucky to have them," Jennifer smiled fondly at Jasper. "And speaking of Lucky, that's the name of our next little girl."

They looked into the stall next to Jasper's. Curled in the shavings was an palomino foal with a cast on her left front leg. She nickered when they stopped in front of the door and scrambled to get up.

"Awww. She's so cute! Can I pat her, please?" Jillian asked.

"Sure. Come on into her stall, and you can give her a scratch."

"How old is this baby?" Grandma Allison inquired.

"She's four months old. She was found walking in the desert out by Lake Pleasant. She was all alone and had an open wound. We think her mother was killed. We looked for weeks and never found her. Thankfully, some hikers saw the baby, and they called us. She was pretty scared at first, but now she is the little princess in the barn, aren't you?" Jennifer opened the stall door for Jillian to go inside.

The little blonde filly was curious, and it was easy to see why she was a favorite. She let Jillian scratch her neck raising her head so Jillian could reach her itchiest spots. "You're so funny! You're just like Jamila. She does the same thing. How long does she have to wear the cast, Jennifer?"

"Oh, she'll be in it for three more weeks or so. She had a partial tear in her tendon, plus some damage the vet thinks was done by a dog or coyote."

"Poor girl." Jillian rubbed the filly on her back, and she turned to get a butt scratch. "Yup," Jillian laughed. "You're just like Jamila. I'm so glad they found her. Lucky is a really good name for her."

"Let's keep the tour going." Jennifer held the door for Jillian and closed and latched it. "Like I said, we keep injured or older horses in here. We are not quite full right now, but that changes every day."

Jennifer led them to the next stall. "Here are a pair of the mini donkeys we got in this week. They were kept by a hoarder on a farm in Nevada. They all ran together in a ten-acre pasture. There were boys and girls who produced babies every year. We worked with a rescue in Nevada to take six of the donkeys. There were more than fifty of them on the property."

"No way. Really?" Jillian couldn't fathom what taking care of fifty donkeys would be like. The two were cute with their long fuzzy ears, soulful eyes, and dark stripes down their backs and across their shoulders.

"I'm afraid so. But good news for the donkeys is that all of them were sent to rescues in Nevada and Arizona, and we only have these two left to adopt. The other four have already found great homes."

"How do you know the homes are good? Do you check up on them?"

"Absolutely. It is time-consuming and difficult to organize, but we check on all of our adoptees. When you read the packet, you'll see that you have to agree to unscheduled home visits."

"Have you ever had to take any horses back?" Jillian wondered.

"Unfortunately, yes. But it isn't a huge percentage. Our agreement states that if you can't take care of the horse any longer, for whatever reason, we get to take the horse back. We just want to be sure they get the forever homes they deserve."

"That's really cool." Jillian grinned at her glad there were people like Jennifer who devoted themselves to helping animals.

"We won't spend too much time by the turnouts since it is getting pretty hot out there, but come and see what we have here." Jennifer walked through the barn and exited the open door at the far end. There were large eight turnouts: four on either side of the center lane. Each turnout had two big shade covers and a big silver watering tub. Jennifer walked to the second turnout on the left.

"Here are the horses that came in with Jamila. I thought you might want to see them." The turnout held eight skinny Arabian horses. Like Jamila, they were only two weeks into their recovery and had a long way to go.

Jillian studied them. There was one grey mare who looked familiar. She was the one who was fussing when they were rescued from Jillian's neighbor. Jillian reached out her hand for the mare to smell and was surprised when she nickered at Jillian's scent.

"Do you think that this mare is related to Jamila?" she asked Jennifer.

"I don't know, but it is very possible. She is approximately twelve years old. We are trying to determine if she was registered. If she was, her offspring might be as well. We've contacted the Arabian Horse Association to find out. I'll be sure to let you know when they respond."

"These are all beautiful horses. Do you think you'll have a hard time adopting them out?"

"Not likely. They are sweet-tempered, and while I don't think any of them have been ridden, they won't be too difficult to train. We find that Arabians are very smart horses, and as long as they are treated kindly, they give their owner endless amounts of love."

"That sure is true for Jamila. She even gives me hugs."

Thinking about all the horses at Healing Horses that needed help, Jillian asked, "What can kids do to help rescue horses? I mean, we are just kids, but can we do something?"

"Absolutely! Kids can do a lot. You can volunteer here at Healing Horses if you want. We have a really neat reading program," Jennifer said.

"Reading program? What do you mean?"

"We invite kids in each week to read out loud to the horses. It helps kids get better at reading, and the horses love it. You can also help cleaning stalls, filling watering tubs, and grooming some of the horses.

"Another way kids can help is to put together fundraising efforts to raise money for horse rescues. We survive mostly on donations. Even if you don't have a lot of money, you can help us at our events or help coordinate and promote our efforts.

"But I think one of the most important things a kid can do to help is to educate people. Tell other kids about the importance of proper nutrition and exercise and vet care. You'd be surprised how many people keep horses without knowing much about them."

"I can do that!" Jillian responded. "I like to read and my friend, Aubrey, loves to read. I bet she would come over with me to read to the horses. And maybe Lila can bake cakes or something to help raise money."

"Those are great ideas, Jillian. All of the help we get here at Healing Horses is important. And of course, you've already done so much finding Jamila and helping that other mare and her baby—although I don't recommend going after mountain lions. Then you called about the horses on Circle Mountain. You're pretty good at rescuing horses already." She laughed. "I wish I had twenty or thirty of you!"

Meanwhile, Aaron was busy implementing his plan. He didn't want to kill the horse. He just wanted to make her sick. Aaron figured that if his mom realized how expensive horses could be, she would say no to Jillian, and they wouldn't adopt the stupid horse, and he could quit looking for work. He felt he deserved more, and he felt sure his sister would want him to have it.

Aaron had been wracking his brain to come up with an idea on how to make the horse sick. He didn't know anything about horses, but the other day he was thinking and noticed their Oleander hedge. He'd heard Oleander was poisonous. All he had to do was feed her a little bit, and she would get sick. No one would ever know it was him. Jillian would be bummed, but heck, life was full of disappointment. He knew that for sure. His mom would change her mind, and the horse would be gone.

Aaron tore off a few small branches of tapered, dark green leaves. He picked a couple of flowers too, not knowing which part was poisonous. He stuffed them in the pocket of his jeans. With his mom, the kid, and that giant idiot of a neighbor gone, he could do whatever he wanted.

Walking onto Bill's property, Aaron felt a little weird trespassing, but it was a fleeting worry. Jamila saw him coming down the drive and whinnied. Thank goodness there were no other close neighbors. He didn't want anyone seeing him with the horse.

"Want a little treat, ya money pit?" he asked Jamila, reaching into his pocket and extracting the flowers and leaves. He held his hand out offering the horse the poison plant.

The horse sniffed and refused. She even backed up. Stupid thing! Aaron thought for a minute and went to the shed. No grain or anything. He would have to find another way. Walking back to the stall, he made sure there was no hay in the feeder, then he headed back home.

Jamila's Thoughts

Eater-anger comes! I see his black lighting. Darkness he swallows. He shows false joy. Offers bad-scented green. Is he good? Trying? Curious?

Don't eat! I know. Memories from inside my inside speak. No. Make ears flat. Back off.

Eater-anger leaves. Relief.

Aaron picked his smartphone off the kitchen table and Googled "homemade horse treats" and found a simple recipe. Feeling sly, he pressed his concoction of raw oatmeal, brown sugar, and molasses around the Oleander flower and leaf, stuffing the remaining plant in his pocket in case he needed it.

She'd never be able to resist this.

Approaching the stall, he arranged his face in a smile and tried talking soothingly as he'd heard Jillian do. "There you go, you dumb horse. Eat the treat, okay? Yeah, there you go," he crooned, reaching out and placing the oat and molasses ball in her feed bucket. He stepped back and waited.

The horse had backed away at his approach, but when he stood back, she stepped forward and sniffed the offering. The tantalizing scent of molasses and oats masked its hidden contents. Aaron smiled as Jamila took up the treat, and nodding her head, began to eat. Laughing, he turned and walked home.

Jamila Continues

He is back.

Is he trying now? Is there love? Sweet-scented richness he offers. My stomach gnaws. He leaks sweet sounds like the Small One, but their color is wrong. His face says joy: light blue joy. Outside. But inside is dark.

Is it good? Rich-scented thick sweet. Curious. Taste is... hiding. Grinding bad parts. Tonguing danger. Do not swallow, Memories wail! I. can't...

Small poison falls, but I have swallowed a black thing. Closer the ground comes. I weaken. Yellow flares. Pain. Panic. Alone. My herd. My Heart. Where? I'm fading! Where are you My Small One? Help me!

CHAPTER 24 - Touch and Go

The ride home from Healing Horses was even better than the ride there. Jillian was thrilled her grandma sounded positive about adopting Jamila. She understood much more now about the responsibility of owning a horse, yet she was unafraid. She wasn't worried about keeping Jamila for her whole life. She didn't want to be without her friend. She felt confident the money she got from her inheritance would cover Jamila's expenses—Jennifer had said so herself.

It wasn't long before they pulled up in front of Grandma Allison's house. "I'll let ya out here ladies," Bill said.

"Can I just go see Jamila really quick, Grandma? You know, to say hi and tell her the good news?"

"I haven't said yes yet!" Grandma Allison insisted, but she smiled when she said it. "Fine. Go on. Be back in half an hour for lunch. Okay?" Jillian nodded unable to keep the suppressed excitement from her eyes.

Bill had barely stopped the truck when Jillian was out the door, calling to Jamila, "Hey, girl! We have good news. Jamila! Jamila?" It was odd that Jamila wasn't standing at the gate where she always was. Jillian frowned. Had the horse escaped? She began to run to the corral. "Jamila? Jamila?"

Bill outpaced her to the stall and stopped abruptly, holding his arm to the side to keep her back. "Wait here," he commanded, and Jillian stopped. When he moved forward, she could see Jamila lying on the ground unmoving.

"Oh, Jamila! Bill, what's happened?" Jillian couldn't stay where she was and rushed through the gate to kneel next to the little red mare. Jamila groaned and began to thrash around.

"Get 'er halter. Now!" Bill's voice was clear and compelling.

Jillian ran to the shed where they kept Jamila's hay and grain, grabbing her halter and lead rope off the hook. She turned and dashed back to Bill who was struggling to keep the mare from rolling over.

"Give it ta me. Thanks." And he slipped the halter over Jamila's head. "We need ta git 'er up an' movin'. We also need ta get the vet here right now. My cell phone's in the truck. Go an' get it. Jennifer's phone number is in there. Call 'er right now, an' I'll git Jamila up an walkin'."

Jillian hurried back to the truck. Her legs felt like rubber. This couldn't be happening! She was just about to adopt Jamila. *It was all going to be fine, and now what if she dies?* She turned on the phone and found his contacts. Jennifer was listed under Healing Horses; with hands trembling, she clicked on the contact.

"Jennifer! It's me, Jillian. You have to call the vet. There is something wrong with Jamila. She was laying down when we got home. She's in pain, I can tell! Oh, Jennifer, please hurry. Bill is trying to get her up and walking."

Jennifer reassured Jillian she'd get the vet over right away, and she would be there too. "Don't let the mare lay down, Jillian. Just keep her moving and help will be there soon. I promise." Jennifer's steady voice helped Jillian rein in her rising panic.

Bill had Jamila up and walking in circles around the corral. He kept a steady pace. If he slowed down, she kept trying to lie on the ground.

"What can I do, Bill? Why is she sick? What could she have gotten into?"

"I want ya ta search 'er stall an; the corral real careful. Look fer anything outta the ordinary. Hopefully, we kin find some clue as ta how she got sick."

Jillian began walking around the corral staring at the ground. There was nothing but sand and a few rocks. She searched Jamila's stall poking in the shavings on top of the rubber mats that lined the floor. She looked in her feed bucket. Empty. *What could have happened?* Jillian fought the tears. She couldn't lose Jamila. She felt a cloak of fear and loss descend like it had when she learned her parents had been killed. She remembered that day like it was yesterday. Playing at Janet's house. Then Mrs. Jenkins bringing her into their living room and the police officer talking to her. Telling her she was alone. Her family was gone. Just like that. And now Jamila. She didn't think she could take it if Jamila died. She couldn't let her die.

Jillian wiped her eyes. She had been staring at the ground seeing nothing but memories. Her tears cleared and the shavings came into focus. And something else: a piece of shiny green. Jillian picked it up. It was a single pointed leaf on a stem with the remains of a little white flower.

"Bill! I think I found something. What's this?" She hurried to catch up with him as he and Jamila strode around the pen.

"Oh, no." Bill frowned as he examined the plant. "I know what that is. She somehow got inta some Oleander. I don't have any growin' at my house. Wind musta brought it here somehow. This here's a poison plant."

Jillian's worst fears were realized. "What can we do? Will she live?"

"We can keep walkin' 'er 'til the vet gets here. We need ta get some Banamine from 'im ta keep on hand here. I could kick myself fer not askin' Jennifer fer some while we were at the rescue today."

Jillian heard an engine and watched as a black truck with an extra big cover on the back pulled in the driveway. A dark-haired man hopped out of the driver's seat, his black-rimmed glasses framed a set of intelligent eyes. "I hear you have a sick horse. I'm Dr. Longton, and this is my assistant, Katie." The tall twenty-something woman with her hair in braids nodded to Jillian and gave her a quick smile.

"I'm Jillian, and Jamila is right over there with Bill. Please take care of her. I'm so worried. We found something in her pen, and Bill thinks she ate Oleander. Will she be okay?"

Dr. Longton took a second to answer. "Let's just see what's going on; we'll do everything we can." He asked Katie to take over walking Jamila so he could talk to Bill. Bill confirmed Jillian's statement, pulling the piece of Oleander from his pocket to show to Dr. Longton.

"I'm afraid you're right. It is Oleander. Usually, we don't see problems until the monsoon season when floods scatter debris everywhere. It's a bit odd to find a fresh piece, but at least we know what we're up against."

Dr. Longton turned to Jillian who was standing with Bill in the center of the corral as Katie walked Jamila in circles around them. "We really have only one option at this point. We're going to tube her with activated charcoal." He saw Jillian's questioning look, and explained, "We take powdered activated charcoal and mix it with water. Then we'll lightly sedate Jamila and pass a tube through her nose into her stomach. We pump the charcoal water through the tube. Activated charcoal helps with detoxification. We may have to tube her more than once. I'm going to get things set up."

Jillian stood in the middle of the corral in shock. She remembered what Jennifer had told her about colic and how dangerous stomach problems could be. She felt alone in the center of chaos: Katie was walking Jamila in circles; Dr. Longton set up a silver bucket, plus gloves, and supplies; Bill pulled a hose to help fill the bucket; and she stood isolated in a cone of silence in the middle of it all.

She felt herself disappear. She was no longer standing in the corral but floating over it helpless and unable to speak. She could only watch the scene from above like a stranger would watch a movie. She knew this feeling. She had this happen before right after her parents died. She hung there, invisible to everyone, observing.

"Jillian. Jillian!" Jennifer's voice sounded close to her ear. Jillian blinked her eyes and found she wasn't floating. She was sitting in the center of the corral where she'd been standing moments before. Jennifer was kneeling down next to her, concern etched on her face. "Are you okay? What happened? You don't look very well. Did you pass out?"

"No, I don't think so. My legs felt weak," she lied. "And I had to sit down. I'm okay now."

Jennifer helped her to her feet. Jamila had been sedated and was standing unsteadily, head down, between Bill and the rail of her stall. Dr. Longton had placed a length of clear tube through her left nostril and into her stomach. She could see him pumping the dark fluid through the tube. Katie held Jamila's head steady. Jillian felt Jennifer take her hand, and they stood together watching the vet do what he could to save her best friend.

The short-acting sedative wore off ten minutes later, and they started walking Jamila again, this time more slowly. "We need to keep an eye on her for a while. I'd much rather

have her at my clinic, but I don't think it's safe to move her."
Directing his comments at Jennifer, Dr. Longton continued,
"We don't know how much she ate or when she ate it. I need
you to look for signs of weakness, tremors, diarrhea, or
difficulty breathing. If you see any of these, call me right away.

"I have an appointment just a few miles from here.
We'll take care of them, and then come back and check on
Jamila. It shouldn't be more than an hour. I gave her a shot of
Banamine to help her relax, and we can tube her again if there
has been no change."

"Is she going to be okay?" Jillian asked, her eyes
pleading for good news.

"It's hard to say right now, Jillian. We'll find out in a
few hours. It's touch and go at the present. I can't promise
anything, but we'll do everything we can to keep her
comfortable and help her get better. Keep walking her slowly.
Let her drink if she wants to—more water is better to help
flush her system. If she wants to rest, that's fine. Just stay with
her. I'm only going to be ten minutes away in case you need to
call. Okay?"

When the doctor and Katie left, Jillian, Bill, and
Jennifer took turns walking Jamila. "You really ought to tell
your grandmother," Jennifer said to Jillian. "She has to know
what's going on. But be sure to tell her that the expense of the
veterinary call is being paid by Healing Horses. You haven't
adopted her yet."

Jillian didn't want to talk to Grandma Allison. She
didn't want to say anything about vet bills and money. She felt
panicked. *What if Grandma Allison thinks it's too expensive?* She
was so worried about the cost of things. *What if she said no, and
Jamila has to go to live at the rescue and got adopted by someone else?*
What would she do? Jillian began to feel distanced from her

body again. She shook her head. She had to stay in the moment.

"Yer granny's gonna find out, honey. Ya should really be the one ta tell 'er," Bill said. She knew he was right. "Don't worry about Jamila. We'll keep walking 'er. If anything changes while you're gone, we'll come an' get ya right away."

"Okay, I guess." Still struggling with the task, Jillian trudged up Bill's driveway toward her grandmother's house. She paused by Grandma's side yard to wipe the tears from her face. Taking a deep breath, she started to the door but then stopped. Something looked familiar. She stared at the hedge by the yard. It was made up of pointed, shiny green leaves and little white flowers. It was Oleander! This must be where the plant that poisoned Jamila came from.

Jillian's heart sank deeper. Was she responsible for Jamila's sickness? Had she picked any of the flowers unthinkingly? She couldn't remember. She was pretty sure she hadn't, but somehow the Oleander had gotten into Jamila's pen. She saw a few fresh leaves on the ground and wondered if the wind had been blowing while they were gone. It had to be the only way.

Grandma Allison was in the kitchen with Uncle Aaron. Lunch was laid out on the table. "Oh, I'm glad you're here, dear. I was about to come and get you. Lunch is ready. Let's eat." She beckoned Jillian to the table.

The last thing Jillian wanted to do was to talk about Jamila being sick in front of Aaron. She knew he didn't want her to have the horse. He would take this excuse and blow it all out of proportion and convince her grandmother not to let her keep Jamila. "Um, Grandma, I need to talk to you. Alone, please? It's important."

"Alone?" Grandma Allison asked curiously.

"Can we please talk outside?" Jillian requested, her eyes filled with concern.

"Sure, honey."

"What's so secret that you can't say it in front a me, kid?" Aaron sneered, his brown eyes intense in their glare. "We're all family."

"Leave her alone, Aaron." There was a fierceness in Grandma Allison's voice. "I need to speak to my granddaughter in private. Go ahead and eat your lunch. We'll be right back." And with that, she ushered Jillian out the back door.

When they were alone, Jillian started talking. She knew she had to say it right out. "Grandma. It's Jamila. She—" Jillian paused.

"What do you mean dear? What about Jamila?"

"She ate some Oleander, Grandma. We don't know how, but some must have blown into her corral while we were gone. I'm so worried. The vet came and put a tube up her nose and into her stomach and pumped in some charcoal water. He's coming back again in a little bit to check on her." Tears slid down Jillian's cheeks. "Grandma, she could die."

The pain in the young girl's voice tore at the old woman's heart. She gathered Jillian in her arms and held her tight, patting her back and telling her it was going to be alright. She felt the girl's sadness so keenly her breath caught in her throat. Disengaging from the hug, she held Jillian by both shoulders and looked at her. "Please try not to worry. Let's go together to see Jamila. It's going to be all right. You aren't alone, honey."

The terms of endearment and the sincere look in her grandmother's powdery blue eyes were too much for Jillian and she hugged her grandmother tight as the tears flowed.

Watching out the window, Aaron was disgusted at his mother's response. The little brat had snowed her again. He couldn't believe it. He watched them walk toward the gate, his mother's arm around his niece's shoulders, hoping now that he'd fed the stupid horse enough Oleander that she would die. If she didn't, well, he'd have to come up with another plan.

CHAPTER 25 - Waiting Game

When Jillian and Grandma Allison arrived at Bill's house, he was still walking Jamila around her enclosure. You could tell Jamila wasn't feeling well. Her eyes were dull and half-closed, and she kept her head lowered as if the effort to raise it was too painful.

Jennifer approached as they arrived. "I'm so sorry that this happened, Mrs. Parker. We can't figure out how the Oleander got in her stall."

"Jennifer, I need to tell you something," Jillian interrupted before her grandmother could speak. "I just realized that we have an Oleander hedge at Grandma's house. That had to have been where it came from. There must have been some wind or something while we were with you this morning. I'm sorry. I didn't know before. I never paid attention to the hedge." Jillian was on the brink of tears again watching Bill lead the despondent mare.

"It's not your fault, Jillian. It isn't anyone's fault," Jennifer said, crouching in front of the guilt-laden girl. "Look at me. Look in my eyes," she said, cupping Jillian's chin. "This was a freak accident. You didn't cause it. Dr. Longton will be back soon to take another look. We're going to do everything we can for Jamila."

"But what if she dies?"

"We are going to do everything possible so that doesn't happen. Okay, sweetie?" Jennifer gave Jillian a hug. Standing to address Grandma Allison, Jennifer explained what Dr. Longton had done to help Jamila so far.

Allison listened intently. This was the kind of thing about owning a horse that she was afraid of. Even when Jennifer explained that Healing Horses was going to pay for the veterinary expenses, she still felt concern. The decision to own a horse was bigger than she imagined. And not just financially.

Allison knew how attached Jillian was to the mare. She had seen a change in her granddaughter's outlook in the short time the little Arabian had been in her life. She knew Jillian would be devastated if the horse didn't make it. *Was it better to just stay away from big responsibilities because of possible problems and heartache? she wondered. Or is it more important to cling to the things that give you joy in life, regardless of how complicated or difficult they might be.*

Dr. Longton and Katie returned minutes later. "How is my patient doing?" he asked Jennifer.

"Hard to tell. She seems accepting of all that we've done. We've kept her walking. She hasn't passed manure yet, so we're waiting for that but no diarrhea either."

"Let me listen to her heart and her breathing. Her heart rate was pretty high last time I checked. Let's check again." Dr. Longton used his stethoscope to listen to her breathing and her heart. "Well, the heart rate is normal now. That's a good sign. Let's see what she does when we stop walking her for a while."

All five humans stood around Jamila waiting to see if she would try to lie down. She looked at them curiously and walked up to Jillian and rubbed her head on Jillian's chest. The girl wrapped her arms around the mare's neck hugging her tight.

"That's a good sign." Dr. Longton offered Jillian a crooked smile. "Let's give her some space and see what she does."

They left the corral and stood at the gate watching. Jamila stayed where she was for a minute or so, and then followed them to the gate. She didn't seem interested in laying down. She wasn't nearly as bright as usual, but she didn't look as sick as she had an hour before. A sigh of relief escaped

Jillian's lips. Grandma Allison put her arm around the girl's shoulders.

"She doesn't seem to be as distressed as she was before," Dr. Longton explained. "The activated charcoal is calming her stomach and absorbing the toxins. She isn't out of the woods, but if she makes it through the next five or six hours without any complications, she should be okay.

"I'm going to give you some injectable Banamine to keep here. She should get a shot at about 4 p.m. It will help calm any stomach spasms and allow her to relax." Dr. Longton turned to Bill. "Have you administered a Banamine shot before?" he questioned. Bill nodded.

"If she doesn't pass manure by 4 p.m., give me a call, and I'll come back and tube her with oil and water."

"Should we keep walking her?" Jillian asked.

"Not anymore unless she lays down and starts thrashing around. The reason we don't want that to happen is she could possibly twist her intestines. If she lies down and is quiet, that's okay. She's probably very tired and still not feeling well. If she wants to nap, that's fine. Just keep an eye on her, and give me a call at four with an update."

Grandma Allison left after Dr. Longton but returned a few minutes later to drop off a platter of sandwiches. They all thanked her. Jillian didn't realize how hungry she was until she started munching her tuna sandwich. They were sitting on Bill's patio with a clear view of Jamila. Dr. Longton had suggested they offer her small handfuls of alfalfa, and she was nibbling half-interestedly on the hay.

"How did you get to work at Healing Horses?" Jillian asked Jennifer while they were eating lunch.

"Well, it is a little bit of a story," Jennifer said. "I was twelve, just like you, when I got my first horse. I didn't come by her in the normal way though. I had a neighbor who wasn't taking good care of his animals. He had a pony, some scrawny chickens, and a few goats. Back then there weren't any horse rescues in Prescott where we lived. Like us, he had a few acres but no barn or shade cover for protection from the wind and rain.

"I used to sneak out in the early mornings and after dinner to pick grass for the pony. I named her Lulu Belle. She was so cute with her blonde, palomino coloring. I'd sneak her apples and carrots as often as I could. I think some days the small treats I brought is all that she ever ate, poor girl." Jennifer frowned at the memory.

Jillian was fascinated. "Was that the Welsh and Arabian pony you told me about when we first met?"

"That's right. Good memory. She was so sweet and willing. She had a beautiful thick tail. I loved brushing that tail." Jennifer's gaze was far away.

"Anyway, my mom knew about my sneaking out, but she didn't say anything to me. My dad started building a pretty good-sized shed in the backyard. He said he wanted room to do some projects. That made it harder for me to spend private time with Lulu Belle. I could see her from my bedroom window, standing at the fence, waiting for me. I don't know why I didn't want my parents interfering with my relationship with her. It doesn't really make sense, but that's what I thought at the time."

Jillian understood. She remembered feeling protective in the same way when she first rescued Jamila.

Jennifer continued, "Then one morning Lulu Belle was gone. I couldn't believe it. She was always in the pasture—she had no other place to go. I was heartbroken. That was the most desperate morning of my life. I was afraid she'd died. I stayed in my room, crying all morning. At noon, my mom knocked on my door telling me to come out and eat lunch. I wasn't hungry at all, but I didn't want to argue.

"Dad was there sitting at the table. Mom served soup. I remember it was homemade chicken noodle—my favorite. I don't think I ate very much when Dad pushed his chair back and looked at me. 'What's the matter, Jen?' he asked me. I didn't want to talk about it, so I told him 'nothing.'

"'Huh,' he said, 'Come outside and help me finish sweeping out my shed.' I was in no mood to clean anything, but I didn't have the energy to disagree, so I followed him. The doors to the shed were closed, and he was talking about stacking stuff. I shut my ears and groaned inside. Then he opened the double doors. There, standing inside, was Lulu Belle! She had a pink bow braided into her forelock. I was in shock. I flew into my dad's arms crying like a baby.

"He and Mom had seen me spending time with her, and Dad talked to the neighbor. I don't know what he said, but the neighbor let him take Lulu Belle. She lived in our backyard for eighteen more years. She was a great, great girl, so patient and kind with me. I rode that pony every day. It was awesome." Jennifer turned to Jillian. "It's going to be great for you and Jamila too."

"That's a cool story. Is that what made you want to rescue horses?" Jillian asked.

"That's the first reason. After college, Lulu Belle passed on. She must have been in her late twenties. It was hard, but I knew I'd given her a good life. I got a job working for the Humane Society helping with fundraising and managing their horse facility in Phoenix until it closed. Then I had the chance to work for Healing Horses as Executive Director and that was three years ago. It has been a rewarding."

The sound of a vehicle approaching interrupted Jennifer. They turned to see Mrs. McKinstry's truck coming down the drive. Jillian was surprised and happy to see Aubrey in the passenger seat. They got out and Aubrey came running up with a look of alarm. "We saw Dr. Longton's truck leaving a few minutes ago, and we just wanted to check to be sure everything's okay."

Jillian's grimaced. "No, it's not okay. Jamila ate some Oleander. I found a couple of leaves in her stall. All we can figure is that it was windy this morning while we were at Healing Horses, and they blew in there somehow. Dr. Longton put a tube up her nose into her stomach. It was awful! She's a little better now though." Jillian suddenly realized that she had never introduced Aubrey to Jamila. "Come and meet her." She led Aubrey to the corral.

Jamila looked up as they approached. She still stood hunched over, looking uncomfortable. While she pricked her ears as they neared, she had none of her normal busy-body curiosity. Aubrey reached over the fence to stroke her neck. "She's beautiful, Jillian. I don't know what I expected, but she really is a pretty horse. Skinny, but still beautiful. Try not to worry too much. I think she's going to be okay," she said, turning to Jillian and hugging her friend. "Really, I have a good feeling. Mom! Come and look at Jamila," Aubrey called, and Mrs. McKinstry joined them at the fence.

"She is very pretty. Great structure. I love her tippy ears and the length of her neck." Mrs. McKinstry appraised the mare. "She has nice large eyes, though you can tell she doesn't feel well. It's quite possible that she is registered."

"Do you think so, Mrs. McKinstry?" Jillian asked.

"I can do a little research if you want. The Arabian Horse Association has a database of owners and their registered horses. I have a membership and can look up the previous owner if you have his full name. Then I can see the horses he has bred and owned. Do you know his full name?"

"I don't, but Jennifer does I bet. I only know his name was Hank." Jennifer heard Jillian mention her name and joined them.

Mrs. McKinstry explained about the database to Jennifer and asked for Hank's full name.

"I will have to confirm the spelling, but I believe his name was Harold O'Conner. He lived up the road. If you can send me the list of horses you find, that would be very helpful. We've requested the information from the AHA but haven't heard back yet."

"Sure, I can do that. How old is this girl?" Mrs. McKinstry asked.

"She's three," replied Jillian, pointing out the bumps on Jamila's bottom jaw.

"We will see if he has a chestnut, three-year-old mare on his list of registered horses. If we find a horse that we think is her, then you can send in her hair for a DNA test to match. Then you'll know for sure if she is purebred, and you'll know her pedigree." Mrs. McKinstry smiled seeing Jillian's eyes light up at the prospect. "I'm happy to help."

At that moment, Jamila grunted. They all turned to look at her and she lifted her tail and pooped. Her grunt was followed with a groan of relief that sent everyone into peals of laughter.

"Sounds like she might start feeling better soon," Jennifer laughed. "That is a really good sign. And it looks like no diarrhea, so that's great."

Aubrey turned to her friend, her eyes sparkling, "You're one of us now. You know, the crazy horse girls that cheer when their horses' poop!"

Jillian giggled and cheered, "Yay for poop!"

"We'd better get home to your sister, Aubrey. And, I'm so glad Jamila seems to be turning a corner," Mrs. McKinstry said to Jillian, giving her a hug. "One thing though, you mentioned wind must have blown the leaves in her turnout, but I was outside all morning at my house and I didn't notice any. Maybe a dust devil kicked them up."

"What's a dust devil?" Jillian hadn't heard the term before.

"It's like a little mini-tornado of dust. We get them around here quite often. Usually, they're only five to ten feet tall, but sometimes we get dust devils that are thirty or fifty feet tall. They spin like a tornado and blow around sand and rocks and whatever they run into. It's best to stay out of their way if you can. I didn't notice any today, but that doesn't mean there weren't any up here. You're a mile away from our house.

"Well, kiddo," Mrs. McKinstry turned to Aubrey, "let's go."

When they had left, Jennifer told Jillian she had to go as well. Bill offered to give Jamila the Banamine shot in an hour as scheduled, but Jillian insisted on staying until dinner. Bill went inside and brought out two sodas. The sound of the snap-hiss as they popped open the cans filled the silence while they sat on the shaded patio watching Jamila.

"Did you hear what Mrs. McKinstry said?" Jillian asked Bill. "About the wind and the dust devils. Seems weird to have them here and not at her house. What do you think?"

"I think the odder thing is there 'aint any other brush or leaves blown round. A wind or dust devil doesn't jus' drop a couple leaves. It stirs up the sand an' the dust an' makes a dang mess. I don't have a good explanation."

They sat for a long while sipping their sodas and pondering the puzzle.

CHAPTER 26 - The Gifts of Giving

Jillian was out of bed and dressed by six-thirty the next morning. She hadn't left Jamila until finally, at 8 p.m., Bill insisted, promising that if anything happened—no matter what time of night—he would come get her right away. Grandma Allison was understanding when she got home, and luckily, Aaron was brooding in his room.

She smelled coffee brewing as she was about to enter the kitchen, but stopped short when she heard Grandma Allison and Uncle Aaron arguing.

"You aren't really gonna let her take in that sick horse, are you? Really, Mom, look what happened already. What if it happens again? Or something worse? How much of our money do we have to waste on that animal anyway!"

"Aaron, it isn't 'our' money. It's her money. A blessing from Josh and your sister. The fact that they paid off my mortgage is proof of their generosity. They planned carefully to ensure Jillian has what she needs. And her emotional well-being is the most important thing to me. Not the money." Grandma Allison's voice rose. "She is your niece. Your family. She's lost everything and has to live here with us—people she hardly knows. If this horse gives her joy and makes her happy, then we're getting the horse. Period. End of story."

Aaron grumbled, "I think you're getting old, Mom. Old and forgetful. Who has helped you take care of this place all this time? Who busts his butt to work, whenever I can find it? Finally, some luck comes our way, and you want to waste it all. I think you're spoiling her, just like you spoiled Janie." Aaron's accusation ended with a whining tone.

"You know very well I did nothing of the sort. I've always treated you and your sister the same way. She was grateful and motivated to get out and do something with her life. If you had wanted to go to college, I would have found a way, but you left before you finished high school. And as far as 'busting your butt,' you have no idea what that really means—"

Aaron didn't wait to let her finish her sentence; he strode to the back door and slammed it behind him.

Jillian thought about what she just heard. Grandma was going to let her keep Jamila! Uncle Aaron would hate it, and he'd probably be meaner to her than he already was, but she didn't care. She took a moment to compose herself before entering the kitchen.

"Good morning, Grandma." She gave her grandmother a hug.

"Good morning, Jillian. Did you get any sleep?" Grandma Allison turned toward the sink not wanting Jillian to see the flush of her face.

"Yeah, some. I'm going to go check on Jamila now. Is that okay? I'll come back in just a little while for breakfast."

"Okay, honey. Be back soon. I'll get some breakfast together. How do scrambled eggs sound?"

"Great, Grandma! Thanks."

Jillian hurried to Bill's to visit Jamila. She was relieved to see the mare standing, head held high and looking much more like her normal self.

"Hey, girl," she murmured, rubbing the chestnut mare on her cheeks and brushing her blonde forelock out of her eyes. "You look lots better today. I'm so happy! And guess what? I think my grandma is going to let you stay with me. I'm so excited." She kissed Jamila on her soft muzzle, the sweet smell of horse filling her nostrils.

Bill had seen Jillian walking down the driveway. He watched as she talked to the horse and kissed her on the nose.

He was grateful Jamila had continued to improve through the night. He'd checked on her every hour until dawn to be sure she was still improving. Bill was exhausted but satisfied he'd done what he could. His brain was fuzzy and his eyes were full of grit. He had been thinking about Jamila all night, and the more he thought about it, the less likely it seemed that fresh Oleander could have landed in Jamila's pen all by itself. Strange.

Jillian checked Jamila's water and hay and headed back home to breakfast. Her grandmother was relieved to learn Jamila was much improved. She had set Jillian's place at the kitchen table and the eggs and toast smelled yummy. Grandma Allison poured herself another cup of coffee and popped two more pieces of golden bread from the toaster and joined her.

"I've been thinking hard about Jamila, and we should talk about her," Grandma Allison said.

Jillian felt the pit of her stomach tighten. "Okay, Grandma." She was scared to say anything until her grandmother went further.

"As you know, I didn't grow up keeping pets. My father felt that all our farm animals needed to have what he called, 'redeeming value.' We had hens for the eggs and meat, and several head of cattle. My parents kept pigs for a while too. Of course, we had a dog and some cats, but they had jobs to do watching over the farm and keeping the mice at bay. So it's difficult for me to completely understand why you want to keep a horse you don't need." Jillian froze.

"But," Grandma Allison continued, "I know how much you love that mare already. I can see she means a lot to you. She is also a huge responsibility, and one that carries great expense." Grandma Allison looked sternly at Jillian to emphasize the importance of her comment. "However, I think you can learn a lot by taking care of Jamila," her eyes softened, "and I know she feels like part of your family now."

"Oh, Grandma. Is that a yes?" Her grandmother nodded with a slow smile. Jillian jumped up and squeezed her grandma in a tight hug. "I can't thank you enough! I promise I'll take good care of her, and I'll save all my extra money in case she ever gets sick again." Jillian felt a lump rise in her throat. She felt her heart swell in a way it hadn't in a very long time. "I love you, Grandma," she said for the first time.

Tears welling, Grandma Allison replied, "I love you too, sweetheart." The embrace they shared felt deep and true. When they separated, they let out a collective sigh.

Grandma Allison began, "I read through the contract and paperwork we got from Jennifer. We will need to complete the application and get you signed up for the classes. They start tomorrow. We'll figure out a way to get you there. Perhaps Bill will be kind enough to give you a ride."

"I'm sure he will. Or maybe Lila will want to go to classes with me. Aubrey already knows lots about horses, so she doesn't have to go, but maybe she'll want to volunteer. It would be nice to be able to help at the rescue," Jillian said earnestly. "I mean, they do an awful lot to help horses, maybe I can help them too."

"Volunteering makes me feel good," Grandma Allison replied. "That's why I go to the food bank to donate my time every week. I always appreciate what I have when I help other people. I think that volunteering at Healing Horses is a great idea." She studied Jillian with great fondness. "Now, go give your friends a call and see if they are going to go along with you. Then we can fill out the paperwork and get in touch with Jennifer."

Jillian dialed Lila's house and learned that she had gone to visit Aubrey, so she called the McKinstrys'.

"I'm so glad you called," Aubrey answered when she got on the phone. "We wanted to surprise you and come by and see Jamila, but—" she paused. "Is she okay? I mean, is she better? Can we come see her?"

"Yes. She's much better. It would be great to see you. I want to talk to you guys about something fun. I'll be at her stall."

Allison had overheard the conversation as she was drying the dishes. She was happy for Jillian that her new friends seemed to really care about her. Now, if she could just get Aaron to let go of his resentment about the horse. She hoped he'd come around in time.

Jillian was grooming Jamila when Mrs. McKinstry's silver truck appeared. Aubrey and Lila hopped out and waved goodbye to Aubrey's mom. Lila hadn't met Jamila yet. "Wow. She is beautiful, Jillian! I can see why you want to adopt her. Did your grandma say anything yet?"

"Actually, we were talking just before I called you. And..." Jillian paused for effect.

"And? C'mon, Jillian, did she say yes?"

"She did. I get to adopt Jamila! I'm so excited!"

"Oh my gosh! That's great," Aubrey gushed. "Wow, you're getting a horse of your own. How cool is that?" Aubrey hugged Jillian, and Lila hugged them both, and they giggled and screamed jumping up and down like little kids.

"Well, I wanted to try my hand at making horse treats, and," Lila pulled a little baggie out of her pocket, "here's what I made. The ingredients are two different types of whole wheat flour—organic of course—and molasses and a little brown sugar. I baked them so they are crunchy. Is it okay if we give her one?"

"I think so," Jillian answered. Lila offered Jamila nugget of crunchy oats. She sniffed the treat and lipped it from Lila's outstretched hand.

"She likes them! You know, I could make a ton of these and we could sell them. I'm pretty sure we could make a zillion dollars, you know. Maybe two zillion." Lila was always full of ideas to make money. Aubrey and Jillian laughed, but Lila had given Jillian an idea.

"So here's what I wanted to talk to you about," Jillian said as they leaned on the rails of Jamila's corral. "As part of adopting Jamila, I need to attend two classes on horsemanship. I was hoping maybe you guys might want to come with me when I go to Healing Horses for class. I know you don't need the class, Aubrey, but they really need volunteers to help, and since you're already good with horses, I was thinking maybe you could volunteer. Then, when the classes are done, we could all go to help them this summer. What do you think?"

Lila answered first. "I'll go to class with you if you want. I'd be interested to learn more about horses. Especially, what they like to eat."

"That's because you are obsessed with food," Aubrey piped in.

"And you're obsessed with books," Lila responded.

"Oh, and that reminds me," Jillian said. "They have a reading program called 'Books in the Barn.' You'd love it, Aubrey. You get to bring a book and read it out loud to a horse."

"You don't really think she can teach a horse to read? I mean, really, Aubs is awfully smart, but..." Lila teased.

Jillian rolled her eyes at Lila. "Of course not silly, but Jennifer says it helps kids learn to read—not that you need to learn anything there, Aubrey—but it also helps the horses to gain trust in people."

"That could be fun. I'll do it. When are classes?" Aubrey asked.

"The first one is tomorrow morning and the next one is on Friday. Do you think one of your moms could drive us? Grandma doesn't drive, and Aaron, well, he is not going to do me any favors. He thinks I shouldn't adopt Jamila." Jillian stopped and frowned. She didn't want to talk about Aaron. "Anyway, it will be great to all go together."

"I can bake some more horse treats tonight to bring with us." Lila got excited.

"And I just started reading Secretariat, so I'll bring that," Aubrey added. The girls made plans for Mrs. McKinstry to chauffeur them back and forth to Healing Horses. "Mom is cool about my horse addiction. She has the same problem," Aubrey grinned. "I bet she'll want to volunteer too."

The girls spent the next hour grooming and playing with Jamila. They laughed and joked and goofed around the whole time.

Returning from the house carrying three bottles of water, Jillian paused. She saw Lila braiding Jamila's mane while Aubrey stroked her horse's neck. She had friends. And a horse! She could barely believe that Jamila was almost hers. Her life had just changed in a big way. Again. The loss of her parents and her move to Arizona had ripped her world apart. She had been lonely and lost, but she now knew that no matter what happened, even the darkest days can be followed by sunshine.

Because of a beautiful chestnut Arabian mare, she had rediscovered her center and a new sense of purpose. She was going to learn everything about horses and help them in any way she could.

Jamila's Thoughts

Oh, great joy! My Small One saved me. Her love is emerald: brilliant and binding. Our herd grows. Life is good for all. There is time for play! And for love. And to be who we are. Together, my Small One and I.

57871731R00133

Made in the USA
Columbia, SC
17 May 2019